FREDDIE MERCURY
HIS LIFE IN HIS OWN WORDS

FREDDIE MERCURY
HIS LIFE IN HIS OWN WORDS

Compiled and edited by Greg Brooks and Simon Lupton
Foreword by Freddie's mum, Jer Bulsara

MERCURY SONGS LTD

OMNIBUS PRESS

London / New York / Paris / Sydney / Copenhagen / Berlin / Madrid / Tokyo

Exclusive Distributors
Music Sales Limited,
14-15 Berners Street,
London, W1T 3LJ.

Music Sales Corporation,
257 Park Avenue South,
New York, NY 10010, USA.

Macmillan Distribution Services,
56 Parkwest Drive
Derrimut, Vic 3030,
Australia.

Every effort has been made to trace the copyright holders of the photographs in this book
but one or two were unreachable. We would be grateful if the photographers concerned
would contact us.

Printed by: Gutenberg Press, Malta.

A catalogue record for this book is available from the British Library.

Visit Omnibus Press on the web at www.omnibuspress.com

For Freddie Mercury
Lover of Life, Singer of Songs

CONTENTS

INTRODUCTION

If Freddie had been alive to participate in this book, he would have had to endure days of tedious interviews with a ghost-writer; another stranger struggling to cajole new insights, who would then have gone away and written a book in Freddie's name. In all likelihood, Freddie would have had neither the inclination nor patience for such an exercise and would soon have lost focus. Freddie hated being bored. With these things in mind, and of course due to Freddie's absence, this book is different in two significant ways.

Firstly, the material herein has been compiled not from just a few days with Freddie, but from interviews spanning 20 years, and myriad sources. The thoughts and opinions he offers are not from one specific time in his life, but from the whole of his professional career. Naturally his outlook and views changed significantly as he got older, and over time these changes are reflected. Freddie's comments on such topics as personal relationships, the other Queen members, songwriting, his private life and plans for the future, altered dramatically over two decades, and thus certain extracts of the text may seem contradictory. This would surely be true of all of us if 20 years of our life were suddenly laid down in print before us.

Secondly, there were no ghost-writers involved in this book. Everything you read will be Freddie's own words – though sometimes it was necessary to tidy them a little. We have not put words in his mouth, nor taken comments out of context. Also, there are several examples of Freddie changing from the present tense to the past tense, and back again, or the reverse of that, but that was genuinely how he often phrased things, and so that aspect too remains authentic. In parallel to that, we have of course amalgamated comments on the same subjects, from various sources and time frames; sometimes explained by Freddie before the event, and sometimes after it, or even during it – the recording of *A Night At The Opera*, for example. Naturally, therefore, the merging of certain sentences or paragraphs may be less than seamless in terms of tense. We made every effort to remain faithful to Freddie's exact words wherever possible and to preserve the integrity of every nuance and sentence – though he frequently began a sentence without ever finishing it! Some of what Freddie said was ambiguous, but it was not our place to try and decipher it. It's up to you the reader to interpret Freddie's words and draw your own conclusions. That is what we believe he always intended.

Whatever Freddie had to say, wherever he said it, and whatever the reason, most of his words, like his song lyrics, thank goodness, were documented and survive in the archive. A considerable proportion of it has been transcribed for the first time ever for this project, and from this amalgamation of everything, Freddie looms larger than life, as vivid as ever, and demanding your attention. There are moments of humour and irritation, of tenderness and startling candour, moments of seriousness and frivolity, and, with hindsight, there are uncomfortable poignant comments too. Freddie addresses each subject in his inimitable flippant way, like no-one else could, but always with good humour and frankness. This truly is Freddie Mercury in his own words, being everything BUT boring. Never boring!

It has been a privilege to research and compile this book. We hope you enjoy it.

Now, without further delay, and before Freddie loses interest, we will, as he often implored his interrogator... "Get on with it!"

Simon Lupton and Greg Brooks, July 2006

FOREWORD

"This book is about my boy, Farrokh Bulsara. Of course, he became better known to the world as Freddie Mercury. But through everything he never stopped being a loving and affectionate son and family member.

I miss him hugely, but thanks to his music he is never far away from me. The talent and intelligence of this unique man – and much loved son – will ensure his memory lives on for generations to come. So I do hope you enjoy reading his own words, for they illuminate the wonderful man he was."

Jer Bulsara

Jer Balsara

Chapter one

I HAD THIS PERFECT DREAM

"I'm not going to be a star, I'm going to be a legend!
I want to be the Rudolph Nureyev of rock and roll!"

In the beginning I was quite prepared to starve, which I did, and just make a go of it. You have to believe in yourself, no matter how long it takes.

When Queen first formed all of us were aiming for the top slot and we weren't going to be content with anything less. You have to have a lot of confidence to get on in this business. It's useless saying that you don't need that. If one starts saying, "Maybe I'm not good enough, maybe I'd better settle for second place," then forget it. We were full of confidence. You've got to have that. You have to have a kind of arrogance and lots of confidence and absolute determination, as well as all the other obvious skills, like music. Arrogance is a very good thing to have when you're starting, and that means saying to yourselves that you're going to be the number one group, not the number two group. We just had it inside us. We all had a very big ego, as well.

We were so stubborn about it. We wanted people to know that we were a band to be reckoned with. And also we had all these ideas to show originality.

You have to start with something outrageous, that's the best way to actually let the public know that you're on the scene. You have to try and get in the public eye – outrage and shock value has always been there. We had our album covers with no clothes on, lots of make-up, black fingernails, and all those things. At that time it was as shocking as anything.

Image is always a very integral part of build-up, I think. Whether it's contrived, or whatever, in the end you form your own instincts about it. It's either a gimmick that hasn't worked, or something that you can play upon. It's all strategy. A certain amount of arrogance and ego, it's all got to be there.

When we first got our band together I think most people were really shocked because they thought pop groups usually consisted of ex-truck drivers of very little brains, who were fed up with being on the dole and had decided to become top of the pops instead. We were one of the bands who were going to take a piece of the action. We were going to do it. We knew we could do it.

We weren't just *playing* with the music scene. We said, "Ok, we're going to take the plunge into rock and we're really going to do a job of it – no half measures." We were still in university and we all had potentially good careers and we weren't prepared to settle for second best if we were going to abandon all the qualifications we had obtained in other fields. We wanted the best. It wasn't a question of wanting world domination, although I know it probably came across as capitalism.

We aimed for the top slot and we were not going to be satisfied with anything less. None of us wanted to get tied to a 9-5 job. I definitely knew that we'd got everything in terms of the music. We were original enough and we started proving it. We weren't the kind of band that would say, "Ok, we're going to do this, but if it doesn't work out we will follow what someone else does." No. That's the wrong way to do it. We weren't going to enter into the music business if we weren't serious enough to go the whole hog. We decided to finish our courses first, which meant one and a half years wait, and if we were still together then, it meant we were serious.

At that time we said, "Let's make it interesting. Let's try to incorporate all the different backgrounds that we've acquired." We weren't snobbish, but we were very careful. We wanted to appear tastefully. Even though we weren't *anybody*, yet, we felt we should appear that way. I suppose it *was* snobbish really. We didn't want Queen to be just *everybody's* band, but for just a select few to start with.

At the start I knew we were going to be huge – and we were. There was never a doubt in my mind. Never. I just knew we would make it and I told everyone who asked, just that. You have to have that kind of confidence in this business. If you like the icing on top, and all the trimmings, you've got to have the confidence to go get it.

I'm the only one in the band from the artistic field. The others are all scientists; Roger from biology, John from electronics, and Brian from physics. Never in my wildest dreams would I have imagined someone like Brian, an infra-red astronomer, would pick up a guitar and be a rock and roller – so there you are!

I went to art school with the impression of getting my diploma, which I did, and then becoming an illustrator – hoping to earn my keep as a freelance. Music was always a sideline, and that sort of grew. When I'd finished with the illustrating course, I was sick of it. I'd had it up to *here*. I thought, "I don't think I can make a career of this because my mind just wasn't on that kind of thing." So I thought I would just play around with the music side of it for a while. Everybody wants to be a star, so I just thought that if I could make a go of it, why not?

And then after a while there is a decision-making time, where you've got to take the plunge; you've either got to say, "I'm gonna go and do this, and just concentrate on this," or not. And we finally did that.

We had to wait a long while – it wasn't just me making up my mind. People like Brian, John and Roger had big degrees to consider. So, some very vital and important decisions had to be made. This is a *full-time* occupation, not a hobby. In a way it was a very good inspiration; we just thought we've left our academic qualifications behind and now we're going to do this. So... there you are! I'm certainly not complaining.

My parents were outraged when I told them what I was up to, but now they see we're making money they seem quite happy about it.

Chapter two

Playing My Role In History

"I've never considered myself the leader of Queen –
the most important person perhaps..."

The concept of Queen was to be regal and majestic. Glamour was part of us, and we wanted to be dandy. We wanted to shock and be outrageous. We didn't want people to have to think about whether they liked us or not, but to formulate an opinion the moment they saw us. We're not just trying to be different, because if you're professional, darlings, you don't have to *try* to be anything!

The idea of Queen was conceived by me whilst studying at college. Brian, who was also at college, liked the idea and we joined forces. The very earliest traces of the band go back to a group called Smile*, who made a single that was released in the States. I used to follow Smile a lot and we became friends. I used to go to their shows and they used to come to see mine. But the group was plagued by bad luck.

I was saying to Brian and Roger, "Why are you wasting your time doing this? You should do more original material. You should be more demonstrative in the way you put the music across. If I was your singer that's what I'd be doing!" Eventually Smile split up and we decided we'd form a band together. It's as simple as that. We thought our musical ideas would blend. Then we met John Deacon [in July 1971] and decided to call the band Queen.

---

* College band comprised of Brian May (lead guitar and vocals), Roger Taylor (drums and vocals), Tim Staffell (bass guitar and vocals). Smile formed in 1968 and disbanded in 1970.

I thought up the name Queen early on. It was a very regal name and it sounded splendid. It's strong, very universal, and immediate. It had a lot of visual potential and was open to all sorts of interpretations. It lent itself to a lot of things, like the theatre, and it was grand. It was very pompous, with all kinds of connotations. It meant so much. It wasn't just one precise label.

I was certainly aware of the gay connotations, but that was just one facet of it. Anyway, we always preferred to think of Queen in the regal sense rather than in the queer one. We worried that the name would give people the wrong idea, but knew our music would override the image because we'd concentrate on putting out good product the whole time. We were confident people would take to us because although the camp image had already been established by Bowie and Bolan, we were taking it to another level. We thought that teenyboppers would probably like us and we might get a bit of a 'pop' tag, but it wouldn't last. At that moment we were just interested in creating a reaction amongst those who came to see us.

There was a long gap between actually forming Queen and having a recording contract. That's why we were so concerned about people saying, "Here comes Queen, glam rock is *in*, and they are following the tradition." We never copied anyone. We were into glam rock before groups like the Sweet and Bowie, and we worried that we might have come too late. Our way was to put together a different kind of theatrical music.

I think when everybody starts off they get a label. Journalists try and put you in a compartment and label you. With any band that starts now, they say they sound a little bit like Culture Club or whatever. We sounded a little bit like Led Zeppelin, because we had harmonies and things, and so they put us in that sort of category. We were labelled so many different things. Labels are as bad as they are good, and if you took them seriously you'd be very silly. I don't care what they say, really. I think people have said things about us and then changed their minds after listening to an album. In the end we had our own stamp – we had the Queen stamp. We had our trademark. A lot of bands that came after us were told they sound like us and they were not very pleased either, but you have to go through that from the start. It's always been that way.

We had a lot of belief to start with, but I thought it would be over after five years and I would be doing something else. It grew and grew, and, remember, we had all been in various bands before, so we had plenty of experience of what not to do, and how not to be flabbergasted by the first rosy offer from record companies.

The moment we made a demo [in 1971] we were aware of the sharks. We had such amazing offers from people saying, "We'll make you the next T-Rex," but we were very, very careful not to jump straight in. We went to probably every record company before we finally settled on one. We didn't want to be treated like an ordinary band. We approached it that way because we were not prepared to be out-of-work musicians, ever. We said, "Either take us on as a serious commodity or don't take us at all."

That's how much planning went into it. It wasn't an overnight success, you know, we'd already been going for three years. We just got the right people to work for us, and the right company, and it took a long time. And yet we were accused of being a 'hype', and compared to bands we'd never even heard of, and then finally told that we didn't even write our own songs.

To most people it must have seemed like an overnight success story, but really we'd been going for a while, doing the club circuits and all that, without having a recording contract. From the very start there were always business pressures of some sort or other. It was like a real obstacle race. I will always maintain the fact that for a major successful band, it's never plain sailing, otherwise there's something wrong about it. If it's too easy you hit your peak and then that's it!

You can't go around saying, "What a wonderful musician I am! What a terrific song I wrote last night!" You've got to make quite sure you get discovered. Part of talent is making sure your music reaches people. You can't just be a wonderful musician and an outstanding song writer – there are lots of those about. Learn to push yourself, be there at the right time and learn how to deal with the business right from the start. That's the state of play in rock'n'roll now. You have to instinctively have an awareness of all the things that will work to make it successful.

The higher up the ladder you go the more vicious you have to be if you want to stop yourself falling off. It isn't that I wanted to be tough and vicious, it's something that is forced upon you. Once you are successful all the baddies move in and that is when you've got to be really strong and try and sift them out – and that is a test of survival really. All the leeches appear and they will suck you dry if you give them half a chance. You have to watch everyone who works for you and if they seem to be taking you for a ride you have to weed them out fast. You can't afford to let anyone get away with anything. It's like playing dodgems; it's rock'n'roll dodgems. You've got to make sure you don't get hit too often by the bad people. Everyone who's successful will always be burnt once or twice. That's kind of a classic rule. Just call it experience.

I think we gained that experience in the early days, getting ripped off and things like that. It's not just a question of having a recording contract and that's it, it's not all going to be peaches and cream. It's a business proposition as well as a musical one. You have to keep in check all of the things that are going on. Talent isn't just about being a good musician, these days, it's about being aware. It's vital to do the whole thing properly. Talent is not just writing good songs and performing them, it's having a business brain, because that's a major part of it – to get the music across properly and profit from it. You use all the tricks of the trade and if you believe in yourself, you'll go all the way. That's the only way we know and it has worked for Queen. And, of course, you must have key people around you to take care of all those things, but you have to take a personal interest as well.

It's very hard to find those kind of people. It's very difficult to put your trust in others, especially with the kind of people that we are. We're very highly strung, very meticulous and fussy. What we went through with Trident* took a lot out of us, so we became very careful and selective with the kind of people that worked with us after that and became part of the Queen unit.

John Deacon kept a very close eye on our business affairs. He knew everything that should and shouldn't be going on. If God had forsaken us, the rest of the group wouldn't do anything unless John said it was all right.

---

* Queen signed to Trident in 1972, a management company owned and run by two brothers, Norman and Barry Sheffield. The band ultimately parted company with Trident, acrimoniously, in 1975.

I think the pressures of the business are getting greater and greater now. There's so much happening that you have to make snap decisions and everything has got to be cut and dried. The most difficult thing to deal with is the time factor, and in some cases you have to make compromises, and we hate that. I just die when I feel I've done that because you're forever thinking you could have done it better, and that's awful. In the end it's *your* career and *you're* the one who has to live with it.

For a band that's starting off, guidance and good management is certainly vital. But people like to think that artists don't have brains, and certainly a lot of them are very easily separated from their money. We were more cunning than that. After Trident, we approached a series of top class managers to make sure we made the right choice. At the time John Reid happened to be the right choice. He flashed his eyes at me and I said, "Why not?" He was great, actually. It was the sort of combination we'd wanted for years. His approach and method of work was so right. He came in to negotiate the whole structure of recording, publishing and management.

Eventually, years later, we became a very difficult group to manage because we demanded a lot. We're fiends, really, and it would take somebody like a Hitler or Goebels to be our manager. Queen is a business, it's an organisation, and we decided to take care of it ourselves.

As Queen play and record together, people see us as having a super-unit image. But Queen is a musical group, not a family. Sure, there are bitter rows, just like there are in many families. We argue about the smallest details. But we all know that fundamentally our aims are very similar; to carry on making good music and stretching ourselves beyond what's been done before by the band.

There's an inward jealousy all the way through our history. Roger, Brian, John and I all write separately and battle to get as many of our own songs as possible onto each album. There's a push, a hunger, a constant fight, which is very healthy. We slug it out and in the end it's very democratic. I don't want to hog things. I mean there is no way I want to say that just I have to write the songs. You have to go only on the strength of the songs. Wouldn't it be awful if I just pushed *my* compositions and insisted they're the best?

It's a kind of a group policy where we argue and say, "Ok, it doesn't matter who wrote it, we think this song is the best, or that song is best, because it works for all of us." I mean, if I pushed a song but was thinking that it might not be a hit, that would be detrimental to me in the long run anyway. So, for example, with *Radio Ga Ga* [1984] I was the first one to say that the song Roger had written was going to be a very good starting point for the single. It was commercial, very strong and different, and very current.

I'm not the leader of the band, by the way. Everybody calls me the leader of Queen, but I'm just the lead singer. I'm not the General, or anything like that. We are all four equal people. We all wanted to be pop stars but the group comes first. Without the others I would be nothing.

Modern-day people in my position call themselves the focal point of the group, which is fine if your name is Rod Stewart and you have a backing band. But no way is this Freddie Mercury and his backing band. When you analyse it, the four of us make the whole thing work. It's 25 percent down the line, and I'm the one up front, that's all. Queen is a four-way thing, but that's very hard, I must say. It's not very easy to get a four-way decision every time, but sometimes you've got to run with the majority. We often disagree. Sometimes we get a two way split, then what do you do? We have to kind of put it in the background for a while and then rehash it later.

We always argued. We fought on virtually the first day. The four of us are very strong individually, so we just keep going at each other. It's like four cocks fighting... and we're the bitchiest band on Earth! We're often at each other's throats. But if we didn't disagree, we'd just be yes-men, and we do get the *cream* in the end. Usually all the vanity, outrageousness and temper is associated with me. I am very emotional, and I certainly get very temperamental, but you would be surprised what you get from the others in the group too. We've all got our individual characteristics, but it's probably that that keeps us together.

I think we've grown so used to each other by now, it's just instinct that keeps us going. Basically, we're four people that work together. There's no big bond and we don't socialise all that often. We've been together so long now that we see each other practically every day anyway, professionally. But I think socially we like to keep away, because otherwise we see too much of each other and we get bored. If there are receptions we need to go to, we do it, we are highly professional in that respect. But otherwise it's nice to just move back into our own thing. The others have their families and of course that takes up their time, and I like to have my privacy without them as well, if you know what I mean.

I can't live a life of one quarter all the time. Because of our work we were always seeing each other, and in anybody's life the same people hanging around all the time would drive you mad. So when the work is finished I go my way, and they go theirs. It can be that I don't talk to them for months and months and then we go on tour and we still gel. It's the music that brings us together, and we have learned to accept each other instinctively now. We know that if we stay together all the time we get on each other's nerves. There was a time when there was a lot of friction, then we sort of ironed that out. Yes we argue a lot and we fight a lot, but in the end what's really the key issue, is that we come up with the product, some good stuff. We use our intelligence. It's very easy to get egotistical and say, "Yes, I'm the greatest!" The egos can run riot and all kinds of things can happen, but you have to keep one foot on the ground. That's called being professional, I guess.

What keeps us going is that musically we still respect each other. We have four very different characters, but that doesn't matter. If musically we don't get on, that's when it starts and tempers fly, but in the end if you can't stand the other person being in the same room, then you have to say, "Forget it!" It's just torture. Instead, when an album's finished, we end up thinking, "Oh well, I had my views, he had his point, but we came together again in the end for the sake of the music."

If you have four very different people in a band like ours, they all want to go off at different tangents, and that's very hard. The break-up of a band normally comes from the fact that one ego seems to shoot too far ahead and then just can't get back. When there is one strong person, the others get left out and think, "This arsehole is just too strong, so we want to try another band." We manage to keep our egos in control one way or another.

That doesn't mean we're all so boring that we agree on everything, but we never let it go so far that we actually say "Ok, let's forget it!" There were times where I thought I should call it a day, but musically we seemed to want to do so much more. I think the reason we have stayed together so long is that nobody wants to leave. If you leave, it's like being a coward. It's a survival instinct that I have in me, and which the whole group has.

Brian was once approached by the band Sparks [in 1975], who said they would like him to join them as guitarist. But we treat that sort of thing as everyday and mundane. We're so involved in what we do that we don't give it a second thought. We've all had offers to join other bands, but while, say, Roger and I would tell them to piss off, Brian takes his time about being nice to people, so they sometimes get the wrong idea. Brian is really too much of a gentleman, which I am not – I'm the old tart... but not for one moment did he consider leaving us.

The only reason Brian would leave Queen is to become an astronomer, not to join another band like Sparks. My God! Especially at the time when it was just starting to be fun. We were riding on the crest of a wave, and things had opened up for us. The rewards were finally beginning to show in the sense that we were being respected as musicians, and our songs were hitting the right kind of people.

I suppose the way we tackled our career sounds clinical and calculating, but our egos couldn't handle anything but the best. I've always thought of us as a top group. It sounds very big-headed, I know, but that's the way it is. When we had the opportunity of playing with Mott The Hoople, that was great, but I knew damn well the moment we finished that tour, as far as Britain was concerned, we would soon be the ones headlining.

We're not scared of trying out different ideas. One of the things that we really steer clear of is repeating the same formula. Basically we are a rock band, and that's what we established with the first album. The second was a bit different, and those who heard the third one didn't even think it was us. You see, the style change has always happened. We go on the pretext that you should stick to the formula that works, so the new phase is still the old style but we add things as they take us. It's just a way of doing things. It goes right through everything – even down to the artwork. I mean, God, the agony we went through to have the pictures taken for *Sheer Heart Attack*!!! My dears, can you imagine trying to convince the others to cover themselves in Vaseline and then having a hose of water turned on them? The end result is four members of the band looking decidedly unregal, tanned and healthy, and as drenched as if they've been sweating for a week. But the point is, everyone was expecting some sort of *Queen III* cover, but this was completely new. It's not that we were changing altogether – it was just a phase we were going through at that time.

There are so many directions our music can follow. I also think that we have just done the things that we wanted to do. We haven't pandered to the public taste or anything. We have tried to be aware what's going on and stay one step ahead. I think in the end it's the good music that speaks for itself and I think we write good songs and we play them well. We did take a lot of risks actually and I think most of them paid off. But we're still as poncy as ever. We're still the dandies we started out to be. We're just showing people we're not merely a load of poofs, that we are capable of other things.

I think every time you make an album it's a new burst of energy – and we make such different albums. When we undertake them it's like a new project every time. It's very fresh, and that's a nice shot in the arm. If we were coming up with the same old thing, thinking it would be readily accepted or whatever, that would be playing safe. We never play safe.

Look at the risks we took with the *Hot Space* album [1982]. It was nice. We were finding out different areas and outlets, therefore we were sort of channelling our energies in different ways. But we were still the same four people, but in many ways it's fresh. I was quite excited. Was the album going to get into the black charts? Was it going to get the disco following? We didn't know.

I remember when *Another One Bites The Dust* came out [in 1980] and went to number one, a lot of people went out and bought it and thought that we were a black act. Then they would come to see our shows and realise we are all white.

I think *Hot Space* was one of the biggest risks we've taken, but people can relate to something that's outside the norm. I'd hate it if every time we came up with an album it was just the norm. It's not to say that we're always right, because we're not. This whole dance/funk mode was basically my idea and it obviously didn't do that well. I think it was way ahead of its time, but we did what we felt like doing at that time and at that time we felt it was right.

We go through so many traumas, and we're so meticulous. There are literally tens and twenties of songs that get rejected for an album – some of them nice ones. If people don't like the songs we're doing at a given moment, we couldn't give a fuck. We take so much care with what we do because we feel so much about what we put across. And if we do an amazing album we make sure that album is packaged right. We're probably the fussiest band in the world, to be honest.

Each time we go into the studio it gets that much more difficult, because we're trying to progress, to write songs that sound different from the past. The first album is easy, because you've got a lot in your head that you're anxious to put down. As the albums go by, you think, "They'll say that I'm repeating a formula here." I'm very conscious of that.

There are so many things we want to do but we can't do them all at the same time. It's impossible. There were a few things that ended up on *A Night At The Opera* which we actually wanted to do on the first album, but it would have been too much to take for most people. You can't cram everything on one album. You have to bide your time.

I enjoy the studio, although it's the most strenuous part of my job. It's so exhausting physically and mentally. It drains you totally. I sometimes ask myself why I do it. After *Sheer Heart Attack* we were insane and said, "Never again." Then look what happened!

25

After that album, we realised we'd established ourselves. We felt that there were no barriers, no restrictions. Vocally we can outdo any band so we thought we would go all out, not restrict ourselves at all, and just do exactly what we want to do. We went a bit overboard on every album, actually, but that's the way Queen is. *A Night At The Opera* [1975] featured every sound, from a tuba to a comb. Nothing was out of bounds. As soon as we made it we knew there were no longer any limits on what we could do.

I'll never forget *A Night At The Opera*. Never. It took the longest time to do out of all the first four albums. We weren't really prepared for it. It was more important to get the album the way we wanted, especially after we spent so long on it.

It was the most important album for us and it had the strongest songs ever. I knew it was going to be our best album. I was really pleased about the operatic thing. I wanted to be outrageous with vocals. At that moment we'd made an album which, let's face it, was too much to take for most people. But it was what we wanted to do. We wanted to experiment with sound, and sometimes we used three studios simultaneously. The actual album took four months to record. Brian's *The Prophet's Song* alone took two and a half to three weeks. There were just so many songs we wanted to do. And it makes a change to have short numbers as well. We had all the freedom we wanted and it was so varied that we were able to go to extremes. I had only about two weeks to write my songs so we worked fucking hard.

The title *A Night At The Opera* came at the very end of recording. We thought, "Oh, we've got all these songs, what are we going to call the album?" It was going to be called all sorts of things, and then I said, "Look, it's got this sort of operatic content, so let's look upon it that way." Then Roger and I came up with the title and it just fitted.

We learned a lot about studio technique from making *A Night At The Opera*. The poor sound engineer really suffered because we wanted as much level as possible. We're very bad for that, actually. We keep pushing the phasers up and he keeps looking at the meters saying, "Oh, it'll never cut!" Then we give him the added task of going over to New York, or wherever, saying, "Make sure that cuts as loudly as possible." It's a very fine dividing line, because we always want to put in more music, but at the same time you've got to make sure you don't put too much in, otherwise it suffers. But our engineer, Mike Stone, was pretty good. That little bugger... what a nice little chap he is!

The other thing that really helped was a successful worldwide tour which we'd never done before. It taught us a lot. It taught us how to behave on stage and come to grips with the music. We started off in Britain [1974] and by the time we took that same stage act across to America, and then to Japan [1975], we were a different band. All that experience was accumulating, and when we came to do *Opera* there were certain things that we had done in the past that we could do much better now. Our playing ability was better.

We tend to work well under pressure. We will work until we are legless. I'll sing until my throat is like a vulture's crotch. We're fussy and finicky and have very high standards. If a song can't be done properly, we'd rather it isn't done at all. We're the fussiest band in the world and we put so much loving into every album. It's what keeps us going. If we were to come up with an album where people said, "It's just like *Sheer Heart Attack* again," I'd have given up. I really would. Wouldn't you?

There will be always be someone new on the scene, a new face after you and your success, and that challenge is good. I think that every major successful band needs that. It's like we are getting a fresh injection all the time. It's good competition and I like that. I mean, when we started we just wanted to knock off who ever we thought were the biggest around, and say that we can do better. There's always going to be other bands that come along, and we're aware of that. I like to feel that I'm competitive. If they're good they'll get there regardless. There's enough room for everybody. Isn't it nice that the newer bands feel that they are in competition with you? Because if you weren't *anything*, they would say, "Oh, forget them!"

The whole punk thing [1977] was a tough phase for us and I thought that was going to be it, but if there is a challenge we embark on it and that's what keeps us going.

27

Actually, I will never forget, we were in the studio doing the *Sheer Heart Attack* track, and the Sex Pistols happened to be in the next studio. You can imagine us and the whole punk rock and anti–establishment thing under the one roof. Anyway, I got Johnny Rotten and Sid Vicious in to listen to one of our tracks and I said that I would sing on one of their songs if they sang on one of mine, and you should have seen them. They were like, "We can't sing with Freddie Mercury!" I was wearing ballet pumps at the time, and things like that. It was quite funny. I think I called Sid Vicious, Simon Ferocious, or something, and he didn't like it at all. I said, "What are you going to do about it?" He had all these marks on him, so I asked if he had scratched himself in the mirror, and he hated the fact that I could speak to him like that.

We don't want to be outrageous. It's just in us. We're the Cecil B. De Mille of rock'n'roll – always wanting to do things bigger and better! But you still have to be talented. Sometimes I think, "Oh my God, they must think I'm working so hard to cultivate all this," but I'm not. I'd hate to live under false pretences. Queen are not frauds. We presented a kind of an image. We weren't putting any labels on it. We said, "This is Queen! This is our music, and this is how we present ourselves." The funny thing about Queen is that no-one can put their finger on it, and we don't want to give it to them. We say, "This is us, and it is up to you to interpret it."

The campness and the flamboyance comes into it too. We like to dress up. If you cultivate something, it is only for the short term, but we are in it for the long term. If tomorrow ballet suddenly became the rage, or jazz enjoyed a new wave of popularity, we wouldn't change. We'd just be playing the same thing, because that's what we really believe in.

When *Seven Seas Of Rhye* was a hit [1974], everybody said it had made a market for us, so let's stick to it. We didn't want that. Our strength is in the music. The amazing thing is we've been around so long, we know how to change, and there's a certain amount of intelligence that goes with it. I know we are good musicians. I know we have the talent to stay in this business just as long as we like. And we take more care over what we are doing than most of the groups who love having a go at us.

We learnt from our mistakes. Now, we don't just go into the studio and make records, but follow everything else through too and make sure it's being done the way we want it. That goes from the artwork on the album sleeves, to the inner bags, and dealing with record companies and management. It's like undertaking a huge project. We still fight though. Brian and I still fight like kids every time we're in the same room... although I haven't hit him yet!

It's hard to pinpoint these things but we certainly have an ingredient between the four of us. We all have a role to play. Queen is like a chariot, with four horses, and at certain times we individually take a turn at holding the reins. We are four different characters, and that's why I think it's worked. No two of us are the same. We all like totally different things, but we come together and it's a chemistry that works. But I couldn't tell you what it is. Who can? It's just something that seems to fit. It's what good bands are made of... and we *are* good!

Let's face it, darlings, we're the most preposterous band that's ever lived.

Chapter three

THE GREAT PRETENDER

*"I often wonder what my mother must think when she sees way out
pictures of me on stage in all that regalia and make up. But like
my father, she doesn't ask any questions."*

My responsibility to the audience is to put on a good show and make sure
they get good, strong entertainment from Queen, and that's that. I have to
make sure that I win them over and make them feel that they've had a good
time – otherwise it's not a successful gig. I like people to go away from our
shows feeling fully entertained, having had a good time. I know it's a cliché to
say "Oh, you have them eating out of the palm of your hand," but I just feel
that the quicker I do that, the better, because it's all to do with me feeling in
control. Then I know that it's all going well.

People want to be entertained in various ways, but the one way I know they
don't want to be entertained, is by people who just come on and casually play
their songs. That's not us. They can hear that on the records. For us, the
strength is in four musicians trying to entertain you. I like to feel that our
songs can take on different shapes depending on what we want to give you.
Something like *Love Of My Life* is totally transformed from what you hear
on the album. It just depends on how we feel when we play them. Besides, can
you imagine doing the sort of things we've written, like *Rhapsody* and
Somebody To Love, in jeans and t-shirts, with absolutely no presentation? It
would never work.

Some bands use backing tapes, but for us trying to mime to tapes just doesn't work. That's not what we're all about and we're the first people to say that if we can't do a number from a record on stage, then we'll forget doing it all together. We don't cheat with tapes, and as far as *Bohemian Rhapsody* is concerned, there was a natural progression there. In the beginning we felt that we were not going to be able to do it on stage, so we just did a few sections of it as part of the medley. Then we were in Boston once and I said, "Why don't we try to do *Rhapsody* as a whole. It's not like we're out there playing our instruments and trying to mime to it." So we tried it a couple of times and I think it's very effective. Now we do it all the time.

I would say songs like *Rhapsody* and *Somebody To Love* are big production numbers – very, very vocal-orientated, which is a very heavy aspect of Queen. That's why *Somebody To Love* is a killer to do live. I tell you, that is very nerve-racking, and the first time we did that song we did it so fast because we just wanted to get it over with. Those kinds of songs have to be arranged differently. I mean how could you recreate a 160-piece gospel choir on stage? You can't. It's impossible.

As far as I know, a lot of the people who buy our records are intelligent enough to realise that all the vocals are just the four of us. Therefore they know that we cannot possibly recreate that on stage, no matter how hard we try. As long as the atmosphere of the song is put across on stage that's what's more important as far as I'm concerned.

All our songs take on a different shape when we do them on stage. A lot of the things we do evolve naturally. It's much better to try and find out what's the best way to do a song, than have preconceived ideas of anything. Otherwise, songs like *Crazy Little Thing Called Love* would never happen.

People try different things, and using a lot of visual theatrics has always been there. All the greatest acts have used them at some time, like Jimi Hendrix and the Stones. It has to be there. Personally I love it because I hate just getting up there to sing. I like to sort of ham it up, and really perform a song. I like to move, and there is a different aggression in each song, so I like to show it. I mean most songs can be performed by somebody just sitting down, but they wouldn't have the same effect or impact. If that were the

31

case we might as well have had cardboard cut-outs of us on stage and just play the album through the PA system.

The thought of doing more lavish stage type things does appeal to me. I like that approach to entertainment and I like that whole cabaret sort of thing. I adore Liza Minnelli – I think she's a wow. But somehow I have to combine it with the group, not divorce from it. That's the difficult thing. We are a bit flashy, but I also think we're sophisticated. It's not glam rock, we're in the show-business tradition.

In the very early days we just wore black on stage, which was very bold. Then we introduced white, for variety, and it simply grew and grew. I dress to kill, but tastefully, and I have fun with my clothes on stage. It's not just a concert you're seeing, it's a fashion show too. I love to change clothes on stage and that's all part of the theatrics. I come on stage after Brian's guitar solo and people know that something is going to happen.

It's just a form of growing up. You get bored of wearing the same costumes and having the same look. I love dressing up anyway. I went from a balletic look to a sort of heavy leather image. The leather influence came from visiting a number of bars in Germany – and, of course, I wear it with panache.

I like leather. I rather fancy myself as a black panther.

In the end we know that the songs speak for themselves and if you had a really crappy song it wouldn't make it sound better just because you were wearing wonderful clothes. I've always thought, "My God! Don't take yourself so seriously." And the first way to do it is to put on a ridiculous costume. Wearing ballet slippers and tights on stage, that's tongue-in-cheek. It was just something that interested me at that point in time. I tried to incorporate it into the stage act, to enhance the music that we played, but if it wasn't working then I wouldn't do it. Besides, I liked the Nijinsky costume. As far as we're concerned, we're putting on a show and it's not just a rendition of an album.

We're rock'n'rollers at heart, but presentation is so important and it's

Proud mother Jer shows off the 7 month old Farrokh in the garden of the family home in Zanzibar (where Freddie was born). These were happy times for the family. While Freddie's father Bomi worked as a cashier in the Zanzibar High Court, the young Farrokh always seemed to be smiling, as can be seen here. Freddie's mother Jer recalls that as a baby Freddie loved to pose for the camera.

That unmistakable smile again, Freddie, centre, lining up with The Hectics (his very first band – at St Peter's boarding school in Panchgani), the quiff and slacks giving little indication of the outrageous stage wear that was to become his trademark in later performing years.

With his band Ibex, Freddie played his first live performance at Queen's Park, Bolton, on August 24th 1969, photographed here. It was during this period that he also changed his name to Mercury. It was originally thought that Freddie named himself after the messenger of the gods in Roman mythology, but this was later corrected by his family who insisted he chose it because Mercury was his rising planet.

With contemporaries at Ealing Art College including Pete Townshend and
Ronnie Wood, it's not surprising Freddie became so intrigued by the
possibilities of a career in music. In his final year at college he joined his
first serious band Ibex. Here he is seen relaxing with members of the group
in a flat in West Kensington, London.

On stage with Queen in 1975. As anyone who ever experienced Queen live in concert will know, Freddie's power and presence in that environment was truly startling – like no other. This image captures a typically confident Freddie in total command of his willing audience… again!

This wonderful image was captured by Brian May at Ridge Farm in 1975, while Queen were recording their fourth album *A Night At The Opera*. It may even be the case that Freddie was working here upon his operatic masterpiece *Bohemian Rhapsody* – or *Rhapsody*, as he so often referred to it. Brian May recalled: "This is one of my favourite pictures of Freddie, in relaxed mode, in Biba t-shirt, creating at a frightening rate whilst we were writing and recording, putting this album together."

Everyone has a favourite period in Queen's career, and *A Night At The Opera* from 1975, the LP that spawned *Bohemian Rhapsody* and *You're My Best Friend*, is a favourite of many fans. This portrait from a photo session of that time captures Freddie during one of the most creative, prolific and exciting periods of his life.

Queen titled their first live album *Live Killers* for very good reason. This spectacular image was taken during the North American *Jazz* tour of 1978, but this same lighting rig featured on the 1979 European tour from which the album came, and captures the colossal energy radiating from stage. The sheer power and enormity of sound, with Freddie at the centre of it all, 'using any device' to thrill the crowd, was a totally overwhelming and unforgettable experience.

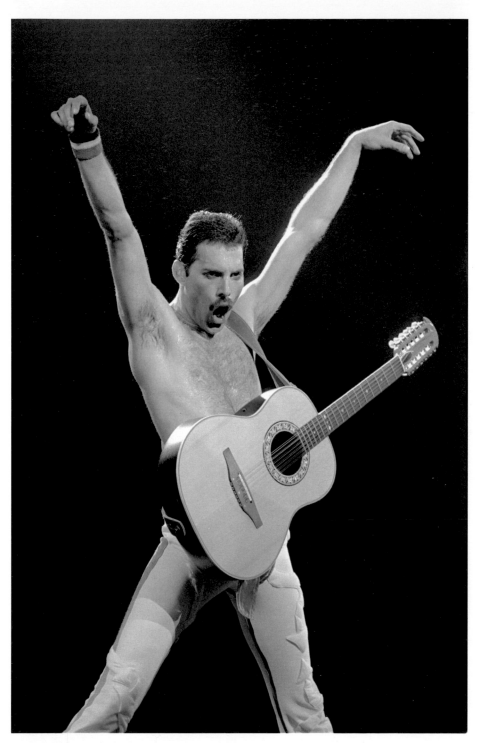

"Ten years ago I only knew about three chords on the guitar, and now in 1982 I know three chords on the guitar!" This was Freddie's preamble to *Crazy Little Thing Called Love* at Queen's June 1982 Milton Keynes Bowl concert - the period from which this photograph comes. That song was the only time Freddie ever played guitar on stage.

With Michael Jackson backstage at a Queen concert in 1980.

something that a lot of groups miss out on. Our act has changed, grown and matured with each tour we've done. We're visually a very exciting band to watch. Our whole set-up is fantastic, and we come on and let it rip. Each new number needs to be expressed visually as well as musically, and we couldn't bear the show to be the same every time. We don't want a lot of props on stage, although we do have a bit of dry ice and throw the odd flower. By the way, we *don't* use steam. One journalist in New York said we used steam, and I had visions of us all boiling kettles backstage.

We think a show should be a spectacle and we've been slagged off in the press for our flamboyant stage show. But that's the whole point. We want to put on a show so we have a barrage of lights and a very complex sound system. But it's all geared to make the music better. People see photographs of us all dressed up and think, "Oh, it's just glam rock!" I feel sorry for people like that because if they had done a bit of homework they would find out what we're *really* about.

Sometimes on stage I'm very near the mark, aren't I? But I have learned to do those kind of things with an air of tongue-in-cheek, where I actually ridicule myself, and the audiences have come to accept it. I mean, who'd get away with coming up to the front rows of the audience and throwing water right in their faces, and things like that? If I was totally serious about it then obviously it would turn sour. But, it's fun really. The one thing that keeps me going is that I like to laugh at myself. If we were a different kind of band, with messages and political themes, then it would be totally different. That's why I can wear ridiculous shorts and ham it up with semi-Gestapo salutes. It's all kitsch. Not everybody realises that.

Once we played a theatre in New York with Mott the Hoople and this particular person wrote that she noticed when I did a costume change, that I changed even my shoes and socks. She also added that she was so close to me she could tell what religion I was, and that I wasn't wearing any knickers! These journalists notice everything down to the pimple on your arse. By the way, there's no coke bottle stuffed down there, my dears. My hose is my own... It's all mine!

I feel incredibly strong on stage and I'm completely immersed in the music. It is awe-inspiring and mind-boggling to be up there with all those people in the palm of your hand. But it never occurs to me that I might have the power to spread political statements among the people. I'm not the Messiah or anything – I don't want to preach to them. No way. I don't want to get bogged down giving them speeches.

In less sensible hands that power could be dodgy. I could cause a riot if I wanted to. You suddenly think, "I've got all this power. I can destroy!" The adrenalin's there, you feel like the devil and it's wonderful, absolutely wonderful. But I know in myself that I would never misuse it. I don't go on stage every night thinking, "Wow! I've got that power." I'm too wonderful for that, darlings!

Sometimes I feel that I could be the Pied Piper of Hamelin, but I wouldn't like to think that people are that stupid. I don't think anybody would follow me to the river... I'd have to drag the buggers. My job is not to teach them, my job is to make music. I don't want to change their lives over night, I don't want to involve the audience in peace messages or anything like that. It's escapism, and I want them to enjoy my music for that period of time and when they don't like it they can just discard the damn stuff in the dustbin. I feel like I'm the master of ceremonies, and that's as far as I like to go because they've come to enjoy themselves and that's all. Entertainment is the key factor as far as I'm concerned, and no way would I like to feel that I'm a kind of political spokesman.

I'm just very frivolous and I like to enjoy myself, and what better way to do it than on stage in front of 300,000 people? I just *cook* on stage! To me, playing in front of a big crowd – that kind of surge – is unequalled. The feeling I get from the audience is greater than sex. I love the excitement of it and I always feel that I want more – more more more. I'm just a musical tart! That's my nature, but that's not what I'm like in real life. When I come off stage it takes me hours to unwind and transform back into my real self. My character is built up of all kinds of ingredients and the Freddie on stage is just one element of me.

Sometimes I feel really evil when I come on stage. When I'm out there I'm in a world of my own. I go up there and have a good time. It's the audience participation that counts, and sometimes I feel I could go into the audience and have a rave – just Freddie Mercury poncing about and having a good time.

I'm so powerful on stage that I seem to have created a monster. When I'm performing I'm an extrovert, yet inside I'm a completely different man. On stage I'm a big macho, sexual object and I'm very arrogant, so most people dismiss me because of that. But I'm not like that really. They don't know what I'm really like underneath. People think I'm an ogre. Some girls hissed at me in the street once, saying, "You devil!" They think I'm really nasty, but that's only on stage. Off stage? Well I'm certainly not an ogre. Of course the stagey streak in me where I love to jump around and be volatile is real, but people don't realise there's a lot more. They expect me to be the same in my personal life as well. They say, "Come on Freddie, *perform*. Give us some excitement."

People seem to think that just because I go tearing around on stage, I should also go tearing around in life. But I don't. This thing about me living a life of excess is so blown out of proportion. I basically have a life of just above the norm, but I'm not at total fever-pitch all the time. I'm not living a kamikaze life. I'm flamboyant, I have a very high energy level and I just like to do things very fast at all times. I can go without sleep for long periods, that's my nature. But you see because of my persona on stage, people think that I carry on that way off stage. If I did, I would have been dead a long time ago.

I don't want people to say that they've seen me on the streets and I act the same way. No no no, they've got to see that a person can change. That's the talent within. That's what makes you something special. You can't portray the same elements that you do on stage, at home in your kitchen, in your household. You have to become a different person so that you can build up to that stage persona, so that it becomes special. Otherwise it would make no difference you coming out of your house and going on stage.

The days are gone when I feel I have to portray that Freddie Mercury image when I'm off stage because of other people's expectations. I found out that you can become a very lonely person if you have to do that, so I'm not afraid to come off stage and actually be myself – which can be very boring and mundane for some people. I'm a jeans and t-shirt man around the house. In fact, when a lot of people meet me they can become very disillusioned because they expect me to be exactly like I am on stage. But I'm a human being and I would like people to realise that I'm bad and good like everybody else. I have the same feelings and the same sort of destructive qualities, and I think people should allow me that freedom. I'd like to feel that I'm being my honest self and I don't give a shit about what other people say.

I want people to work out their own interpretation of me and my image. I don't want to have to say, "*This* is what I am." I think mystique, not knowing the truth about someone, is very appealing, and the last thing I want to do is give people an idea of who I actually am. That's why I play on the bisexual thing, because it's something else – it's fun.

Of course I'm outrageous, camp, theatrical and dramatic, but I haven't *chosen* that image. I am myself, and in fact half the time I let the wind take me. I'd have been doing myself an injustice if I didn't wear make-up because some people think it's wrong. Even to talk of being gay used to be obnoxious and unheard of, but those days are gone. There's a lot of freedom now and you can put yourself across in a way you want to.

I always want to play to as many people as possible. The bigger the better! I think everybody that wants to be successful and is successful wants to play to the biggest audiences and I'm not afraid to speak out and admit that. I want to reach as many people as I can, and the more the merrier. As far as I'm concerned I'd like the whole world to listen to my music and I'd like everybody to listen to me and look at me when I'm playing on stage.

Being the support act was one of the most traumatic experiences of my life. When you support another artist on tour there are so many restrictions. You don't get your own light show, your playing time, your effects. There's no way you can show the public what you can do unless you headline and you know the people have come to see *you*.

The first time we went to America was as support to Mott The Hoople, and it acted as a 'breaking-the-ice' tour. We got a taste of America and so we knew what would be needed the next time we went. We believed it was the music and not gimmicks, and we felt our music had something sufficiently different about it – some originality and versatility. Our record company in America [Elektra] weren't billing us as the 'Next Big Thing'. They said, "Have a listen to this. This is British rock in the royal tradition."

We had a few setbacks. We were there to follow up the *Queen II* album which had taken off, but at the height of the tour Brian fell ill with Hepatitis. He actually had the illness for about six years without knowing. Anyway, the cancellation of the tour was a shock and we thought it was a big loss. Yet we still managed to do a month, and if we hadn't gone at all they'd have probably thought we never existed. Of course, a whole tour would have helped us a bit more, but we never thought we had 'lost our chance.' We knew that the time was right for us there and that we'd go back pretty soon. You should have seen the write-ups; they were beautiful, and they just wanted us to come back as soon as we could.

The next year, when we had finished the European tour, we went back to America, which was quite a bash. It was for two months and that's when I came a cropper. I had voice trouble and I thought it was just a sore throat. It really started hurting, especially after we did six shows in four nights. But these horrible nodules had begun to form on my vocal chords. I went to see specialists and they were talking about an operation. They were going to give me laser-beam treatment where they just singe them off. But they didn't know about the after-effects, which could have been dangerous. In the end they told me I'd have to stop singing or I'd have no voice left at all. That really frightened me so we had to cancel quite a lot of shows.

In America we seemed dogged by bad luck. On tour there in 1975 a young American tart got into my hotel room and pilfered my jewels and bracelets. She was just evacuating the room when I accosted her by the elevator. I pulled her by the hair, dragged her back into the room, emptied the contents of her bag and everything but the kitchen sink came out. I retrieved my things and said, "Get out, you Seattle slagbag!"

A year later my very promising pop career nearly came to an untimely end. Two young girls outside the theatre decided to claim my scarf as a souvenir. They quite forgot it was wrapped around my neck at the time and nearly strangled me. I'm sure Her Majesty doesn't have to put up with that sort of thing, but then she never had anything in the charts did she?

I always loved touring in Japan, particularly with all those geisha girls – and boys. I loved it there, the life style, the art. Wonderful! I'd go back tomorrow if I could. We knew it was going to be really exciting as soon as we landed. As we walked into the airport building, we couldn't believe our ears. They had stopped all flight announcements and were playing our music instead. It's an incredible feeling to step into a country already filled with fans, and we all hoped we could live up to it.

At the time *Queen II* was the LP of the year, and the hysteria started the moment we got there; riots at the airport, bodyguards, just like the old Beatle days. The organisation was spellbinding, and we loved every minute of it. We needed protection because you couldn't go down into the lobby of the hotel as it was infested by really nice people waiting for autographs. We each had a personal bodyguard and mine was called Hitami. He was the head of the Tokyo bodyguard patrol, and his entire job was to pamper and cosset me throughout the tour and make sure no harm came to my person. He was very sweet and gave me a lovely Japanese lantern, which I treasure.

We also went to a tea ceremony, like the one the Queen went to, and I remembered how she pulled a face after two sips. Basically, it's a thick green liquid and it's bitter as hell! You're supposed to finish it in three sips. Afterwards we went to a reception and all the top Japanese businessmen were there, as well as the British ambassador and his wife. She told us, "We went to see Led Zeppelin, but he was so loud!"

At the concerts I couldn't believe the crowds, all milling about, swaying and singing. We've been very lucky that everywhere we've been there has been a very similar kind of reception – where the audience get very in-tune in terms of how to participate. Later, wherever we did *Love Of My Life* they instinctively knew that they had to sing it. It's amazing to watch. I didn't have to tell them, they just automatically knew their role. I like an audience to respond like that. Maybe we'd like them to sit down and listen to some of the songs sometimes, but I get a lot more from them when they're going wild, and it brings the best out of me.

Yes it was a heavy tour, but it put us in a different bracket over night. It's a tour we had to do and it meant after we'd done it we could do the next British tour on our own terms, exactly how we liked. To start with we were booked in well beforehand at semi-big venues, but by the time we came to doing them we had the new album out and we got a bit of TV exposure and everything escalated. I think if we'd waited we could have done all the big venues – it was just a matter of timing. But I'm glad we did the tour when we did, even though there was a lot of physical and mental strain.

It's great being on tour and getting on that stage in front of a collection of people who have never seen you before. You have to start from scratch and you're playing every song like it's a new piece, and it's lovely. You also have to use all your old tricks because we're always interested in creating a reaction amongst those who come and see us. I am over the top and there are things in my stage act that I know will get a certain reaction. I was once thinking of being carried on stage by Nubian slaves and being fanned by them. I was going to audition them and personally select the winners. But where to find a Nubian slave?

Basically, people want art, they want showbiz, and they want to see you rush off in your limousine. That's why we view albums and concerts as two different spheres of work. There's a different feel in the studio as compared to when you're on stage and when we're up there before an audience where we can really let loose. We set ourselves a very high standard and 99 per cent of the audience wouldn't agree with our assessment of a gig. We all scream and shout at each other and destroy the dressing room and release our energy. We end up rowing about everything, even about the air we breathe. We're always at each other's throats. One night Roger was in a foul mood and he threw his entire bloody drum set across the stage. The thing only just missed me – I might have been killed. Another time Roger accidentally squirted Brian in the face with his hairspray in a tiny, steaming dressing room and they nearly came to blows. It was all good fun though!

I think Queen had really developed its own identity by this point. America saw that we were good, and so did Japan, and we were the biggest group in Japan. I don't mind saying that. We could outdo anybody because we'd just done it on our own musical terms. We knew if we just did something that's harmonised we'd be called the Beach Boys, and if we did something that's heavy we'd be Led Zeppelin again. Instead we always liked to confuse people and prove we're not really like anyone else. If anything, we have more in common with Liza Minnelli than Led Zeppelin. We're more in the showbiz tradition than the rock'n'roll tradition. We had an identity of our own because we combined all those things that define Queen. That's what people didn't seem to realise.

We were learning all the time, and you're only as good as your last performance. We all wanted perfection and to make our show more polished. It doesn't always work out like that though. Many is the time I dashed off stage for a costume change and heard Brian finish his guitar solo abruptly, while I'm still putting my trousers on, so I had to rush back on stage half-undressed. I was caught out quite a few times like that.

We felt that as long as we had a sense of achievement and that we were breaking new ground, we were happy and ought to continue. They wouldn't let us into Russia mind you, they thought we'd corrupt the youth or something. We wanted to play where rock music had never been played before. It was for that reason we went to Latin America [1981] and in the end we opened South America to the rest of the world. If you crack it there, the amount of money you make can be tremendous.

We went to South America originally because we were invited down. They wanted four wholesome lads to play some nice music. By the end of it I wanted to buy up the entire continent and install myself as President. The idea to do a big South American tour had been in our minds for a long time. But Queen on the road is not just the band, it involves a vast number of people and costs a lot of money for us to tour. In the end we said, "Fuck the cost, darlings, let's live a little!"

I knew a lot about Argentina, but I never imagined that we were so well known there. I was amazed by the nation's reaction to our being there. We were all terribly nervous because we had no right to automatically expect the works from an alien territory. I don't think they'd ever seen such an ambitious show, with all the lighting and effects we use.

A whole lot of journalists came from all over the world to see us play in Argentina and Brazil. In Sao Paulo we played to 120,000 one night and 130,000 the next night. It had never been done before, and it was all very new to them. They were worried that with such a vast audience it might become political, and they pleaded with me not to sing *Don't Cry For Me Argentina*. They had the Death Squad there to protect us, the heavy, heavy police who actually kill people at the drop of a hat, in case the crowd became unruly. And before we came on stage the whole military was up front with bayonets.

We were actually taken from one place to another in armoured vehicles that were usually used for riots. My dears, it was the most exciting bit of all. There were six motorcycle police roaring in front of us, ducking and weaving in and out of the crowds and traffic just like a display team. The van had holes in the side for the police to stick their guns through; and there we were, screaming out of the stadium in the most dramatic way. It was fantastic.

Rio, in 1985, was wonderful. It was mind-boggling to be up there with all those people in the palm of your hand. During *Love Of My Life* I stood there blinking away like mad and swallowing hard, with the same feeling that The Last Night Of The Proms gives me. The sunshine makes such a difference and people are allowed to flower there. They were a wonderful audience and I loved their displays of emotion.

They get over excited sometimes and there was a bit of trouble when a fight between some of the crowd and a cameraman broke out. It was during *I Want To Break Free*, because in the video for that song we had all 'dragged up'. So I came on stage with false boobs under my vest, and a vacuum cleaner, to bring that image back, and they went a bit mad. At first I thought my boobs were too big for them. The trouble was when I first tried them, in Brussels, at the start of the tour, some people who work for me said that at the back of the arena you really couldn't see them – unless they're twice the size of Dolly Parton. So I had to get some bigger tits. I don't know why they got so excited about me dressing as a woman; there were lots of transvestites there – just go and look on any street corner and you'll find them.

I certainly didn't go on dressed like that to provoke them and I may have been stoned like the Queen of Sheba, but I wasn't giving up my boobs for anyone!

I was the one who wanted to stop touring and change the cycle that we'd been going through for so long. If we carried on touring I wanted to do it for totally different reasons, I'd had enough of those bombastic lights and staging effects. I didn't think at my age that I should be running around in a leotard any more. I tell you, I felt the after-effects of touring, it was as if I'd done a marathon every night. I had bruises everywhere.

So before we started the Magic tour [1986], I was actually quite worried because I knew my own limitations and I thought the audience was going to expect me to do the same kind of thing I'd always done. I thought, "My God! I have to go through all that again." And once you're on tour you can't make any excuses. It's not like the early days when I could do anything because I always knew that I could get away with it. Now everyone's watching.

I've put on a little podge, a little bit of middle-age spread, and the moment they see a little bit of that they're going to start calling me 'Fatty Mercury'. I had to think about all that and make sure that I was perfectly fit. But even then no matter how much you do beforehand, you only know if it's going to work the moment you do the first show, and by then it's too late because the whole tour's already been planned, and venues booked.

We've always thought if we weren't able to put on the kind of show we wanted, then it wasn't worth doing. I hate this process of doing a show and making excuses afterwards. That's bullshit. Once you do a show you've got to stick by it.

I was also really worried because my voice takes a beating. The more vocal gymnastics I do in the studio, the more I have to do on stage, because if I didn't, people would say, "Oh, he can only do it because he's got the studio," and I hate all that.

I like to have the freedom of the stage and run around a bit, but when I saw the stage designs for the Magic tour I thought, "Oh my god! What am I going to do? I'll need roller skates to go from one side to the other." I didn't want to let anyone down, so at first I just didn't want to do the tour. But I think it's all in the mind. Even though I thought I should go and do all this training, in the end I just thought, "Oh fuck it! I'll just *will* myself into it." So I did a few press-ups and although the first three or four shows were agony, my muscles started working and after that and it was fine. I'm glad I did that tour because it was one of the most successful tours that we'd ever done and I'm glad I took the plunge.

My voice has been giving me problems since the first years of touring, because we used to do really extensive tours and sometimes even matinees. Can you imagine me doing a matinee, dears? I ended up getting nodules, uncouth calluses growing in my throat, and from time to time they harmed my vocal dexterity. It's misusing the voice that does it and once you get nodules they are always there, and they always come back.

There was one instance, a show in Zurich, I think, where I actually dried up on stage. I thought, "My God what am I going to do?" I could hardly speak, nothing came out and it was just an awful feeling. Normally I can fake it, but you can only fake it to a certain degree and after that it becomes ridiculous. So I just said, "Fuck this!" and walked off leaving the other three on the set. I'd never let my public down in that way before. Some way or other I've always gotten past that stage and finished an entire show. But I had to do it, and I was really pissed off. Ever since that happened it's been a recurring nightmare for me. If it happened once it could happen again.

Sometimes with dry ice, the heat from the lights doesn't allow it to rise, and I have to sing through a fog. It's just the hazards of being on the road but it's so frustrating because you want to make those high notes. Instead you're singing an octave lower because you don't want to chance it, and croak.

There were a few phrases where I opened my mouth and nothing came out. The others were very sympathetic, but I mean what can they do? They can't scream and shout at me and say, "You *have* to have a voice." They helped me a lot. Sometimes when I came to a high note I just opened my mouth and Roger sang it. Roger sings very well and Brian does too. They were my crutches when I needed them.

My nodules are still with me so I have to go easy on the red wine, and to warm up I do what I call 'mock operatics.' I do it naked, though, because there's a certain piquancy about that. With clothes on, it doesn't work, so I sing in the complete raw.

I went to throat specialists, I think I saw them all, but they always tell you to just rest and not do the tour or have an operation. I came very near to having an operation but I didn't like the look of the doctor and I was a bit perturbed about having strange instruments forced down my throat.

I always get depressed and upset when a tour stops. Suddenly you're back home and you have to will yourself back into the pace. You have to make your own cup of tea again and I'm used to being pampered and cosseted, my dears.

In the end I want people to see me as somebody who sings his songs well and performs them properly. I like people to go away from a Queen show feeling fully entertained, having had a good time. They are pure escapism, like going to see a good film. After that, everyone can go away and say that was great, and go back to their problems.

Chapter four

THE MASTERSTROKE

*"We have been forced to make compromises before,
but cutting up a song will never be one of them."*

Bohemian Rhapsody was something that I'd wanted to do for a long while, actually. It wasn't something I'd given much thought to on previous albums, but I just felt that when it came to the fourth album I was going to do it.

It was really three songs and I just put them together. I'd always wanted to do something operatic, something with a mood-setter at the start, going into a rock type of thing that completely breaks off into an opera section – a vicious twist – and then returns to the theme. I don't really know anything about opera myself, just certain pieces. I wanted to create what I thought Queen could do on that theme. I wasn't trying to say that it was authentic opera, certainly not – it's no pinch of *Magic Flute*. I wasn't saying I was an opera fanatic and I knew everything about it, I just wanted it to be opera in the rock'n'roll sense. Why not? It was as far as my limited capacity could take me.

I like to think that we've come through rock'n'roll, call it what you like, and there are no barriers. It's open, especially now, when everybody's putting their feelers out and wanting to infiltrate new territories. That's what I've been trying to do for years. Nobody's incorporated ballet. I mean, it sounds so outrageous and so extreme, but I know there's going to come a time when it's commonplace. It's something I'll try, and if it doesn't work, well it doesn't work. I'll try something else.

Rhapsody needed a lot of thought, it didn't just come out of thin air. Certain songs require that sort of pompous flair. I had to work like crazy. I just wanted that kind of song. I did a bit of research. Although it was tongue-in-cheek and it was mock opera, I still wanted it to be very much a Queen thing. I'm really pleased about the operatic thing. I wanted to be outrageous with vocals because we're always being compared with other people, which is very stupid. If you really listen to the operatic part there are no comparisons, which is what we wanted.

You want some trade secrets? Ok. It was quite a mammoth task actually, as it was done in three definite sections and just pieced together. Each one required a lot of concentration. The opera section in the middle was the most taxing because we wanted to re-create a huge operatic harmonies section between just the three of us – Brian, Roger and myself singing. That involves a lot of multi-tracking and things. I think between the three of us we created a 160 to 200-piece choir effect.

There was a section of "No, no, no!" to do, that kind of escalating thing, where we just sat in there going "No, no, no, no, no, no, no!" about 150 times. Those were the days of 16-track studios. We have 24 and 32 tracks now, and even more than that. We did so many overdubs on the 16 tracks for that song, we just kept piling it on and on, that the tape went transparent because it just couldn't take any more. I think it snapped in two places as well.

It took a *lot* of work. I had everything in my mind and I made Roger, Brian and John play passages where they were saying, "What the hell is happening here?" It was things like just one chord and then a long gap, and they were saying, "This is ridiculous!" But I had it in my head what was going on around each segment. It took ages to record.

I'm going to shatter some illusions now. It was just one of those pieces I wrote for the album – just as part of writing my batch of songs. In its early stages I almost rejected it, but then it grew.

It was just a phase we were going through at the time. I think there was a lot of good timing and some luck. It was the *Night At The Opera* period

46

[1975] and we were writing like crazy. There was so much hunger there – a push, a hunger, a constant fight, which was very healthy. We had so much that we wanted to bring out. Yes, we went a bit overboard on that album, and on most albums, actually. In certain areas we always feel that we want to go overboard. If something is worth doing, it's worth overdoing!

A lot of people slammed *Bohemian Rhapsody*, but who can you compare it to? Name one group who have done an operatic single. I can't think of anybody. But we didn't do an operatic single because we thought we'd be the only group to do it, it just happened.

Rhapsody was an era, it was of its time. The time was right for that track then. To be honest, if we released it today I don't think it would have been such a big hit. I'm not being modest; the feeling was right then for that kind of majestic recording. I just think that if it wasn't written and I was sitting here today, I wouldn't write it now because of my awareness of what's going on at the moment. That's why I also write things like *Body Language* [1982]. I don't consider *Body Language* to be that much beneath *Rhapsody*, if you know what I mean. I think it's just as good but in different ways.

If people think because of that huge success I'm going to suddenly revert and come out with a rehash of *Bohemian Rhapsody* again, they're mistaken. There's no way I'm going to do that. You have to keep coming up with something fresh, keep coming up with the goods. If you can't come up with the goods when it's needed, then forget it. You can't live on your past, and I can't live on *Bohemian Rhapsody* all the time.

We look upon our product as *songs*, we don't worry about singles or albums. All we do is pick the cream of the crop. We look upon it as a *whole* to make sure the whole album works. With *Bohemian Rhapsody* we just thought that it was a very strong track and so we released it. But there were so many arguments about it. Somebody suggested cutting it because the media reckoned we had to have a three-minute single, but there is no point in cutting it – it just doesn't work. We just wanted to release it to say that this is what Queen is all about at this stage. This is our single, and you're going to get an album after that.

The choice of single is always very difficult. There's no such thing as a sure-fire hit. I'd say something like *Rhapsody* was a big risk, and it worked. We started deciding on a single about halfway through making the *Opera* album. There were a few contenders. We were thinking of *The Prophet's Song* at one point, but then *Rhapsody* seemed to be the one.

It had a very big risk factor. The radio people didn't like it initially because it was too long, and the record companies said they couldn't market it that way. After me having virtually put the three songs together, they wanted me to slice it up again. Can you imagine? The six-minute length could have meant that radio stations would have refused to play it. People were saying, "You're mad! They'll never play it. You'll only hear the first few bars and then they'll fade it out." We had numerous rows. EMI were shocked... "A six-minute single? You must be joking!" they said. But it worked, and I'm very glad.

There were lots of talks of cutting it down to a reasonable air-playing time, but we were adamant that it would be a hit in its entirety. We have been forced to make compromises before, but cutting up a song will never be one of them. Why do that when it would be to the detriment of the song? They wanted to chop it down to three minutes but I said, "No way! Either it goes out in its entirety, or not at all. It either stays as it is, or forget it!" It was either going to be a big flop or people were going to listen to it and buy it and it would be a big hit. Luckily it became a major hit.

It's a consensus between the four of us. We have to actually fight it out. We made the right decision with *Bohemian Rhapsody*, but this is not to say that we were always right because we're not. It could have gone completely the other way, dears.

It was a strong song and a mammoth hit on the continent. That was really when the volcano erupted, when it suddenly just went bang! That single sold over a million and a quarter copies in Britain alone, which is just outrageous. Imagine all those grandmothers grooving to it!

A risk element is always involved and that's the way I like it. That's what makes good music. We've always taken risks. And that is one way of proving to people that we believe we have the confidence behind a song – we believed in it. I felt, underneath it all, that if *Rhapsody* was successful, it would earn a lot of respect. It was a song of extremes and I think its success or failure would have been in extremes. It certainly paved the way for us, and brought us to a much wider cross-section of the market. Actually, I think our music is becoming even more versatile, so we can please a pretty wide range of people now. And the people who have come to see us in concert have spanned a wide age group.

We've always put our necks on the line. We did it with *Queen II* in 1974. On that album we did so many outrageous things that people started to say, "Self-indulgent crap, too many vocals, too much everything." But that is Queen. After *Bohemian Rhapsody* they seemed to realise that that was what Queen were all about. They finally got it!

People do seem to regard that song as our peak, because they just think in terms of, "How are Queen going to follow that?" But they're only looking at it in terms of sales. Yes that's one way of looking at it, but as far as I'm concerned, in terms of song writing and studio technique, we've bettered ourselves already.

People still ask me what *Bohemian Rhapsody* is all about, and I say I don't know. I think it loses the myth and ruins a kind of mystique that people have built up. *Rhapsody* is one of those songs that has a fantasy feel about it. I think people should just listen to it, think about it, and then decide for themselves what it means to them.

I hate actually trying to analyse my songs to the full. You should never ask me about my lyrics. People ask, "Why did you write such and such a lyric and what does it mean?" I don't like to explain what I was thinking when I wrote a song. I think that's awful. That's not what it's all about.

I don't like to analyse it. I prefer people to put their own interpretation upon it – to read into it what they like. I just sing the songs. I write them and I record and produce them, and it is up to the buyer to interpret it the way that he or she feels. It's not up to us to come up with a product and label it. It would be so boring if everything was laid out and everybody knew exactly what it was all about all the time. I like people to make up their own minds. I think if I were to analyse every word, it would be very boring for the listeners and it might also shatter a few illusions.

I think that song is like a sort of lynch-pin or something for us. That's the way I see it. It suddenly opened up a new area for us. I thought, why not take it? Go with it! Suddenly you're moving at a very rapid pace. Sometimes you can move too damn fast, and I think you miss out on something that you've actually created.

Of course I'm proud of *Bohemian Rhapsody* in one sense. I'm proud of a lot of things. The thing I'm most proud of, of all, is the fact that I'm still around after all this time. That takes the cake to be honest!

Chapter five: part one

AN AMAZING FEELING

"When I was a small child, in the choir in India, I just loved to sing.
I didn't look upon it as a career, I never thought about it in those terms.
Then I realised I could actually write songs and make my own music.
It dawned on me that I could do it my way.
Suddenly there was a little taste of success, and I liked it."

I have no set rules for writing a song. It's haphazard. Some songs come faster than others. I never sit down at the piano and say, "Right, I've got to write a song now." No. I feel a few things out and get some ideas about them and then I begin. It's hard to explain but there are always various ideas going through my head. Certain things just come together, but others I have to work for. It sounds conceited, but something like *Killer Queen* came to me in just one day. It just fell into place, as some songs do. I scribbled down the words in the dark on Saturday night, and the next morning I got them all together and worked all day Sunday, and that was it – I'd got it. Whereas, other songs I had to really work at to try and get the lyrics. *The March Of The Black Queen* [1974] for instance, on our second album, that was a song that took ages to complete. I wanted to give it everything, to be self-indulgent.

I've been known to scribble down lyrics in the middle of the night without even putting the light on. I like to think that I write songs in lots of different ways, depending on my mood. *Crazy Little Thing Called Love* [1979] I wrote in the bath. It took me five or ten minutes to write. In the studio, I did that on the guitar – which I can't play for nuts, and in one way it was quite a good thing because I was restricted, knowing only a few chords. It's a good discipline because I simply *had* to write within a small framework. I couldn't work through too many chords because of that restriction, and as a result I wrote a good song – I think. If I'd known too many guitar chords I might have ruined it.

I'm always thinking about the new songs I'm writing. I can't stop writing new songs. I have a lot of ideas bursting to get out. It comes instinctively. I just like to write nice little catchy tunes. It's just something that I have to keep doing, but I do enjoy it too. It's a kind of hobby in a funny way. It's so rewarding in the end that you just want to keep doing it and explore different aspects of it to see how they turn out. It's like painting a picture. You have to step away from it to see what it's like.

As far as lyrics go, they're very difficult. I find them quite a task. My strongest point is melody content. I concentrate on that first, then the song structure, then the lyrics come after. The structure of the melody comes easy to me, it's the lyrical content that I find difficult. I have to work on that part of it. I sometimes feel that my melodies are so much stronger than my lyrics, that the lyrics bring them down. I think my melodies are superior to the lyrics quite often. I hate writing lyrics. I wish somebody else could do it. I wish I had a Bernie Taupin. Mind you, I'm not like that, I like to do it all myself. I'm a greedy bitch.

When I'm writing songs I just have to be left alone on my own, locked up. I have to be left alone so I can concentrate. When I write a song I'm very strong about the whole content within it. If it works, it works. When I'm not thinking about it, that's when it happens best. I like to capture a song very quickly so that it's fresh, and then you can work on it afterwards. I hate trying to write a song if it's not coming easily. It either comes quickly, and you have it, and I say, "Yes, we have a song," or if it's not happening, I normally just say, "Look, forget it."

I write a song the way I feel it, and I'm always willing to learn. It's so much more interesting to write different types of songs rather than repeat the same formula. I seem to write songs that I don't think about much at the time, but which seem to sort of catch up on me, if you know what I mean, afterwards.

So I guess without knowing it, it's a sort of subconscious thing. I think most people write songs that are inside them. I'm not one of those writers that practices trends and says, "Ok, this is trendy today, let's write a song about that." I just like to do different things, and not repeat myself. I don't like to stay in one position for too long, so that comes out in my songs and lyrics. I like to try everything once and I'm not scared of pitfalls. I love the challenge and I like doing things that are not part of the mainstream. I'm not afraid to speak out and say certain things in my songs because I think in the end being natural is what wins.

I'm not blowing my own trumpet, but sometimes I do churn them out quite quickly. It can come easy if I put my mind to it. I turn songs out far quicker than the others I think. People ask me, "How prolific a writer are you?" I write a dozen a day, dears!

If you put them all into one *bag*, I think my songs are all under the label *emotion*. It's all to do with love and emotion and feeling. It's all about moods. Most of the songs I write are love ballads and things to do with sadness and torture and pain, but at the same time it's frivolous and tongue-in-cheek. That's basically my whole nature, I guess. I'm just a true romantic and though I think everybody's written songs in that field, I write it in my own way, with a different texture. Basically I'm not writing anything new, I'm not sitting here trying to say, "Look, I've written a song that nobody else has written before!" No. But I do it from *my* point of view.

A lot of people have fallen in love and a lot of people have fallen out of love, and people are still doing it, so I'm still writing songs about that – in different atmospheres. I think love and the lack of love is always going to go on, and there are so many different ways that people fall in and out of love. I think most of my songs seem to follow that path, and I think to sing and write about love is actually limitless. I think I'm writing things that everyday people go through. I feel I've gone through all those things myself too, so basically I'm encompassing and actually gathering that research and putting them into songs. I'm a true romantic, just like Rudolph Valentino. I like writing romantic songs about love because there's so much scope and also they have so much to do with me. I have always written those. I mean, since the early days, since the second album, and I think I will always write those things because they are part of me. I like to write all kinds of different songs, but the romantic ones will always be there. I can't help it, it's just automatic. I'd love to write songs about something totally different, but they all seem to end up in a very emotional and tragic way. I don't know why. But still there's an element of humour in the end. So that's basically what my songs are all about.

It's quite funny, actually; my lyrics and songs are mainly fantasies. I make them up. They are not down to earth, they're kind of airy-fairy, really. I'm not one of those writers who walks out onto the street and is suddenly inspired by a vision, and I'm not one of those people that wants to go on safari to get inspiration from wild animals around me, or go up onto mountain tops, and things like that. No, I can get inspiration just sitting in the bath. I am one of *those* people. I don't need wildlife for inspiration. I'm not the kind of person who is generally inspired by a particular scene, or by art, as such, although there was one example on *Queen II*, with the song *The Fairy Feller's Masterstroke*, where I *was* inspired by a painting I saw. That is very, very unusual for me. Being arty, or whatever, I go to art galleries a lot and I saw in the Tate Gallery this picture by Richard Dadd, who was a Victorian artist I liked. I was thoroughly inspired. I did a lot of research on it and what I tried to do was to put the words into my own kind of rhyme, but I was using his text, as it were, to depict the painting – what I thought I saw in it.

Inspiration strikes anywhere. It strikes when I'm least expecting it and it plays havoc with my sex life. Some of my songs have even come to me in bed. But I have to write it down there and then otherwise it's gone by morning. One night, when Mary [Austin] and I lived together, I woke up in the middle of the night and a song just wouldn't go away. I just had to sit down and write it, so I got up and dragged my piano over to the bedside so I could reach the keyboard. That didn't last long – she wouldn't put up with it. And I can't say I'm surprised.

There are many things that influence you to make music, you know, almost all that surrounds you. In my case, it might be that I'm going somewhere and I have an idea, and I keep it in mind, but basically I sit at the piano and tinkle and tinker away. A few ideas might come to me and I try to remember them, and then I come back to it at a later stage and try to put it all together. Sometimes I will simply sit at the piano and I suddenly get an idea and then I try to work the song out. Maybe I force myself to get ideas in a sort of direction sometimes, or I leave them alone and come back to them a month later and suddenly they fall into place. But there's not some big inspiration. They are all different. It sounds like such a come-down to some people, because they hear the fantasy content and they think, "Wow! I wonder what inspired that?" They've probably got some great vision in mind. There is no strict format that I stick to. Sorry to disappoint you.

We all have our own ideas on how a song should be, because a song can be done in so many different ways, depending on who is doing it. Sometimes you can see something else in other peoples' songs. We will sometimes all help each other, so that's what takes a lot of time. Most of the songs are developed in the studio these days, whereas before we used to have 'routine' time. These days there is no time for anything, so we just book studio time and we go in there. Sometimes that takes a while because we spend studio time writing songs when we should be recording.

There's a different way of writing now. Before, I used to sit at the piano and really work my arse off to get all the chords and the whole construction before I turned a theme into a song. Now it's a different way of thinking. Lately I've written songs on the spur of the moment. In fact I go into the studio totally unprepared and I think, "Oh, what am I going to do this time?" And suddenly the basic idea comes out and I think, "Let's do it." It might be totally atrocious, it might be abysmal, or there might be one or four bars that I think are nice, and I can pick up on that. Or, I'll just leave it there and go back and work on it later.

I compose on the piano, or I can compose in my head as well. I write the song around the melody most of the time, although sometimes a lyric will get me started. *Life Is Real* [1982] was one of those, because the words came first in that instance. I just really got into it; pages after pages, all kinds of words. Then I just put it to a song. I felt that it could be a Lennon-type thing. That song is an ode to John Lennon, in my limited way. Very seldom do my lyrics come up first but I just had this pattern of lyrical ideas and I wanted a surreal sort of feel in that. They came to me in Houston, believe it or not, when I had a few days off from my Mexican stint – on the Queen tour. I thought, "Why not? I can do it. I'm a musician." Listening to a lot of John Lennon songs, I just thought I could try and create a kind of atmosphere that he created. So therefore I actually fought to get that kind of oriental violin sound on that – a sort of weepy feel – which I love doing. I tried to put across the surreal kind of lyrics, which is what, to me, John Lennon was. He was larger than life, I think, and an absolute genius. Even at a very early stage when they were the Beatles I always preferred John Lennon's things. I don't know why. He just had that magic.

I don't want to change the world with our music. There are no hidden messages in our songs, except for some of Brian's. My songs are like Bic razors; they're for fun, for modern consumption. People can discard them like a used tissue afterwards. They can listen to it, like it, discard it, then turn on to the next. Disposable pop.

I don't like to write message songs because I'm not politically motivated – like John Lennon or Stevie Wonder. Politics enters into my thinking, yes, but I discard it because we are musicians. I don't like to be political and I don't believe that I have a talent to write deep messages. Music is very free. It just depends on who you are. I mean John Lennon can do that, but I can't. My songs are just like commercial love songs and I like to put my emotional talent into that. I don't want to change the world or talk about peace because I'm just not motivated that way. Politics isn't my thing at all. I'd ruin a country. Can you imagine it? I'd sing all my speeches!

As far as I'm concerned I write songs which I think are basically... *fodder*. I've said this before. Songs are like buying a new dress or shirt; you just wear it and then you discard it. Yes a certain few classics will always remain, but as far as I'm concerned what I've written in the past is finished and done with. Okay, if I hear it on the radio or people talk about it, I feel that's great, but to me I'm thinking about what they are going to say about my new stuff. I write them, and I leave them. If you asked me to play some of my older songs on the piano now, I couldn't. I forget them. I learned them for the time. Before playing them again I have to go in a day earlier and try to work out all the chords... to my own songs. I forget them very quickly. For example, *Love Of My Life* is adapted on stage for guitar, but it was written on the piano. I've totally forgotten the original, and if you asked me to play that now I couldn't.

I think our music is pure escapism, like going to see a good film. It's for people who can go in there, listen to it, forget their problems for a little while, enjoy the two hours, and that's it. Come out again and go back to their problems, and come back for some more next time. Really, it should be like that. That's what theatre and entertainment should be. I don't like to infiltrate into the political areas. We don't have hidden political messages in our songs, it's just not the way we are. We are an international group and we like to play to every audience, anywhere. We don't go to different territories in a political way. We're just an English rock and roll band that plays music for everybody.

My music is not channelled into any one category. I don't want my songs to be heard by a certain intelligent quota, I want everybody to hear it because it *is* for everybody. It's an international language. I don't write music just for Japanese or just the Germans, it's for all ears. Music is limitless. I'd like the whole world to listen to my music. I'm not an elitist.

I'm not here to announce, "Change your life through a Queen song!" I can't get up in the morning and say that I'm going to write a 'peace' song, that wouldn't be right because those sorts of things you actually have to believe in. I'm not saying I don't believe in peace, I just don't feel that I am personally capable of writing peace messages. I don't want to put myself in that environment. I'm into writing songs about what I feel, and I feel very strongly about love and emotion. The John Lennons of this world are few and far between. Certain people can do that kind of message thing, but very few. Lennon was one. Because of his status he could do that kind of preaching, and affect people's thoughts. But to do that you have to have a certain amount of intellect and magic, together. People with mere talent, like me, have not got the ability or power. You could be sure John Lennon and Stevie Wonder meant it when they wrote a peace song, because they lived accordingly, but I'm not that way. For me to write a peace message would be wrong and people wouldn't be able to relate to it – me suddenly writing about peace and saving the world. You have to go through a certain amount of history for people to know that you believe in what you are writing about, and as far as I'm concerned I hope that people do believe that I go through torture and pain in terms of love. I think that's my natural gift, so that's all I want to do in my songs.

To be honest, I would never like to put myself on a par with John Lennon at all, because he was the greatest as far as I'm concerned. It's not a matter of having less talent, just that some people are capable of doing certain things better than anybody else, and I feel that I'm not equipped to do the things that Lennon did. I don't think anybody should, because John Lennon was unique, a one off, and that's the way it is. I admire John Lennon very much and that's as far as I want to go. I just want to put myself across in my songs in the best way I can.

When I heard that Lennon was dead, I was shocked and dumbfounded. What do you do? Words fail me, to be honest. It was something that you think could always happen, to somebody else, or to you, or whatever, and then it did happen to somebody, and it was John Lennon. There was shock and disbelief.

When John passed away and I wrote that song in tribute, it was just from me to him, and there is no parallel between anything he did, and what I did. It was just a little gift, you know, because he passed away. *Life Is Real* wasn't a message song, it was just a song in tribute to the man, which is completely different from what John was doing.

If I were pushed, I *could* write a message song. I'm not going to say that I have never written a message song, but it's not in the John Lennon idiom, not in that trend. I mean, I wrote a song called *We Are The Champions*, which is a kind of message anthem, but not for world peace. It's in a different direction.

Having said all that, on my solo album, *Mr Bad Guy* [1985], I wrote a song called *There Must Be More To Life Than This*, and that is probably the nearest thing I could cite to a message song – and that's not even a message as such. It's the nearest I want to go to in terms of talking about world politics or the disasters that are happening in the world. I don't really like writing songs in that sphere, but there comes a time when I feel emotional in that way and it's just a very small part of what John Lennon actually did. I'm being very modest, but very true.

I hate trying to analyse my songs to the full. You should never ask me that. My lyrics are basically for people's interpretations. I will say as much as I can about certain songs I write, but in the end I don't like to pull a song apart because I don't even analyse them myself – I just sing them. I write them and I record and produce them and it is up to the buyer to take it the way that he or she feels, otherwise I ruin a kind of mystique that might portray that track. I hate doing that.

People say, "Why did you write that lyric and what does it mean?" I don't like to explain what I was thinking when I wrote a song. Does it mean this? Does it mean that? is all anybody wants to know. Fuck them, darlings! I will say no more than what any decent poet would tell you if you dared ask him to analyse his work. If you see it, dears, then it's there. *You* interpret it how *you* want to. There's no great big message. I try to conjure up something and get that into a song, and then I hope that people will try to make up their own minds about it – which is a good thing. That's what I like to feel when I listen to somebody's album.

I like people to put their own interpretation on my songs. Really they are just little fairy stories. I've forgotten what they were all about. It's just fictitious – fantasies. I know it's like bowing out, or the easy way out, but that's what it is. It's just a figment of my imagination. I think if I were to analyse every word, it would be very boring for the listeners and it might even shatter a few illusions.

A lot of people are creative, in their own way. It doesn't have to be just in music. That is part of talent as well – do you see dears? I've always maintained that, that you can't just sit at home and say, "Look, I'm so wonderful, I'm so creative, I'll just wait." No. You've got to go out there and actually grab it, and utilise it, and make it work. That *is* part of talent.

Having talent is one thing, but to actually use it and feed it to the masses, is another part of talent. It goes hand in hand. It's called Hard Sell I think. You've really got to sell your arse. You've got to go in there and ram it down their throats and say, "Here I am! I'm creative! I'm wonderful! Here... EAT IT!" You have to do that. If there are other ways of doing it, then my God, you tell me.

Is it still possible to write good and original songs? Oh I should bloody well think so! I should hope so. Oh yes. No matter how great the competition, there is still room for originality and good songs. Of course. I think there will never be an end to good song writing. There'll always be good writers and people writing good songs – depending upon how the media takes them and how they look upon it. I think there is still room, but it's getting more difficult. There's still room for originality and writing good stuff, yes. There's lots of room for classics – and I do my best.

I can't go on forever writing and scrambling out totally different ideas, because you can go neurotic. It's always in the back of my mind. I write a passage and I think, "Oh! This sounds a bit similar to this one." But that's the wrong way to look at it, although it's there. Take for example from a harmonising point of view, the harmonies; we've done them backwards, inside out, every way, and there's not many areas left, so it gets harder and harder to be original all the time, but we are constantly striving for that.

I know people can actually dry up, in terms of writing songs. I know people who have. I think about that sometimes. I think maybe one day I'm just not going to be able to write as well as I do now, but it hasn't happened yet so what can I do? I want to write better songs. It's my career, it's my project in life. I don't wake up every morning and think, "Oh, have I dried up?" At the moment... I've been very prolific. And you know, *He's* looking after me, so I'm OK. That doesn't worry me. It's just something I don't think about. *Other* people think about that. When it happens, I'll deal with it. It won't happen. That's all there is to it. I don't think it'll ever happen. I'll die first.

One of the things I want to do is to try and spend time writing a musical. I think the time has come. In terms of solo projects, I did one solo album, *Mr*

Bad Guy, in 1985, and the project with Montserrat [Caballé], in 1988, but now I want it to be more than an album, so I'm going to try to do a musical. I know it will take a while but it would be my solo project so I can get involved in the actual script and the whole thing. I can write songs that are sung in the actual storyline rather than just seeing a film then writing a song that fits it, afterwards. So it's a big project and I'm thinking about it quite a lot at the moment.

Also, I have visions of actually having a film made of my life story, one day, which I would have a key part in. I might not play the lead myself. My dears, the things I've done in my lifetime... it'll be totally triple X-rated, I'll tell you!

There's no way to tell if someone writes a better song than you, because in the end it's up to the public. The only way you realise it's good, is if it's received well.

You don't know what it means when you write a song that people actually appreciate and they say it's a good song. It's a wonderful feeling!

If my music makes people happy, that's a wonderful thing. That makes me very happy. If some of that, even if just a little trickle of it comes across to the people, then that's fine. And if people hate it... tough shit! They can go and buy somebody else's record. I'm not going to lose sleep or come up in a rash if somebody says, "Oh my God, that's terrible!" I'm too long in the tooth dears.

Chapter five; part two

WRITING AND RECORDING
WITH QUEEN

"The fighting for the Queen songs has been one of the
worthwhile factors. Sometimes I think it's a question of
who ever fights the longest wins the day."

Basically we get back home after a tour and we know that in a couple of months time it will be time to record a new album again. We go our separate ways for a while, and write individually, and then we get together and play each other our ideas. And that's when we try to work out which ones are going to go and which will stay. We try to work out what kind of an album it's going to be. That's what the last few albums have been like; individual songs from individual writers. We have a teething period when we get together – a long sifting process, with a lot of rows, where we pick the best songs. It's not only about how an individual song is concerned, it's also about what will go, what will work best, and how the other songs will sound with each other. So it's basically looking in terms of an album, as opposed to just individual songs.

I think we are aware of current trends and changes and we write accordingly. I mean, Brian still writes in a heavy mould, or whatever, but I think the four of us write very different songs, which is good. The more we write, the further apart in song writing we become and the repertoire grows. I think we are accumulating more and more research and spanning different territories in that way. I'm writing very different stuff now to what Queen were doing say three years ago.

It's quite competitive now, just within the band – before it even gets out to the public and becomes competitive with all the other groups around. The whole band is very particular. We don't go in for half measures and I'm pretty hard on myself. There are no compromises. If I think a song isn't quite right, then I'll discard it. There are four good writers who are equally adept at doing things, and there are no passengers, especially now that Roger's writing very well and so is John. Brian and I used to be the principal writers, but now we all write. There's a good fight right at the start of every album, where we present the material and say, "Ok, what do you think?" and then the real fighting starts.

You can have the best musicians in the world but that doesn't make a better song. It is entirely up to the song and the person that writes it. You have to fight. I like to add my two penn'orth, dears. If it was made too easy for me I would come up with lesser material. Because we fight, it makes it much more interesting and you get la crème de la crème, the cream of the crop. The fighting for the Queen songs has been one of the worthwhile factors. Sometimes I think it's a question of who ever fights the longest wins the day.

I've said it before, but the way I see it is that you write songs and once they're out, they're out, and then you just move on. If the new album is a flop, we'll just move on to the next. We've had albums that haven't been absolutely *major*, in the past, like *Jazz* [1978], but we just moved on. That one was considered to have taken a slight dip, but that didn't stop us. We came up with another album, *The Game*, and that was huge.

If I was to think about it in those terms, where I woke up every morning and said, "Are they going to like everything?" I'd have heart seizures and ulcers. I like to think of it in a more broader spectrum than that. It's to do with longevity too.

I'm quite aware of what goes on, but that doesn't mean I want to incorporate that particular trend into my songs. I still write a song the way I feel it, and if that means that it needs something old fashioned, I will do it. I will never let a song down, the song comes first. I feel so strongly about my songs that if they are not done properly, I'd rather they weren't done at all.

63

That's why something like *Living On My Own* [1985] has got scat singing in it, something like Ella Fitzgerald did a long time ago – and not a current trend. Maybe it could set a trend today, because a rock'n'roll artist has never done scat singing before in that way, and it might not be appreciated, but I'm not worried about that. I wanted to showcase my vocal ability on that track and that's what I was doing. So, I do whatever I like. I'm aware of what goes on but that doesn't necessarily mean that I'm going to pinch it.

A lot of reviews I've read lately have said, "If you associate Queen with the *Bohemian Rhapsody* harmonies and that kind of Cecil B. De Mille package, forget it, because there's not an ounce of that on this record." In a way that's quite nice. It's either black or white. In this case, with *Hot Space*, I think it is a big risk and the public have been torn between two. I hope the Americans will see it as something new, because the other side of the spectrum is that England just totally ignored it. It was obviously not their cup of tea. So they just rejected it totally.

I'm extremely upset – outraged, in fact. I just think they could have given it a little... I mean, I know *Body Language* [1982] was the first one of its kind from us, but it met with such disapproval in England. God! If they think that because of that situation I'm going to suddenly revert back and come out with a rehash of *Rhapsody*, they're mistaken. There's no way I'm going to do that. But I'm glad that the Americans have seen that side of it.

Good songs don't have to be absolutely saturated with humungous operatic scenes, or what have you. I really think that part of talent these days is not just being a good musician, and writing a damn good song, it's also being aware of what's happening out there and getting with the pace. And after that, you really just leave it to the luck of the draw.

I feel that Queen have written some good songs which *haven't* sold, but to me they are still good. Songs are only perceived as good as long as they sell and get into the charts. I want to write commercial music that sells to everybody. If I think I have written a good song that doesn't sell, I say, "Okay, forget that, just throw it out and onto the next!" I just move on to the next one.

With Rod Stewart at a party in 1975.

With Meatloaf, backstage at the LA Forum, USA. September 1982. Queen performed two sell-out concerts at that venue on the 14th and 15th.

With the incomparable Billy Connolly at the playback
gathering for the 'Flash Gordon' album, December
1980. And with Gary Numan at the same event.

With Alice Cooper,
at a party in 1977.

Freddie enjoying champagne with two of his closest
friends, Elton John and Peter Straker, in 1978.

With Mott The Hoople singer Ian Hunter and radio presenter Bob Harris, both good friends of Queen, at the playback of *A Day At The Races*. Advision Studios, London, November 1976.

With actress Jane Seymour at the Fashion Aid charity event, Royal Albert Hall, London, November 5th 1985.

With the inimitable and equally colourful Boy George (lead singer of Culture Club), for whom Freddie had great respect, at the same event.

Freddie and Cliff Richard at the Roof Gardens party, July 12th 1986, celebrating the massively successful Magic Tour, and two sell-out shows at Wembley Stadium. Less than a month after this photograph was taken Queen would perform what would be their very last concert, at Knebworth Park, Hertfordshire, August 9th – though no-one knew it at the time!

A curious Freddie with an unknown party guest in Rio de Janeiro Brazil, January 1985.

With Dionne Warwick backstage at La Nit Festival, Barcelona, October 1988, at which Freddie and Montserrat Caballé performed songs from their newly released *Barcelona* album.

Relaxing in Munich in 1985. During this period Queen were working upon the Bob Geldof-inspired *One Vision* single at Musicland Studios, and then sessions for the album that became *A Kind Of Magic*. It was a frenetic period for the band, although Freddie also found time to speak at length with writer David Wigg again during this period – parts of that conversation feature in this book. In addition to all of this, Freddie was concluding work on his first solo album at this time.

The trademark of Queen, and which I like, just happens to be a coincidence – that there are four writers who write very different material, which gives us maybe a wider span than most other groups. We are equal, but I have been the main writer from the start. If you go back to the very early days, Brian and I have been the main songwriters. John and Roger didn't write at all to begin with, so Brian and I took up about fifty percent of all the song writing. We have grown up being the two main writers, but then the others started writing and we encouraged them.

I don't think there has ever been an album where it was completely equal writing status. On the last album we came very close, but I think maybe for the next album the time has come where it will be completely even in song writing.

If we were writing all the same kind of songs then we would have got fed up long ago, but we were all writing different songs, so that kept us interested. If everybody wrote the same kind of thing that appealed to the same kind of people, then it would be a bit boring. We have four totally diverse personalities and different egos, and that's good. We still fight! We still fight like kids. A Queen album is made up of that. You have to fight. I think that's the best way. I like to fight for the very best we can achieve, and I think I make everyone else fight as well. It makes it much more interesting.

Sometimes I'll take one of my songs to Brian and he may put guitars on it the way he wants to, not my way. So we'll fight. Sometimes we're the bitchiest band in the world. There's a lot of bad vibes, but in the end it always comes together. We have to conflict, otherwise it would be dull, I think. Sometimes you just disagree, but in the end what does happen is that the writer is the boss. He can say, "Look, this is the way I want the song, and this is the way I'm going to have it." As far as I'm concerned the person who wrote the words has effectively written the song.

In the early days, Brian and I always wrote far more, as I've said, but now it's come to the stage where they all want to pull their weight. I think that at this point in time, that's the only way for Queen to survive. I know people think that I hog everything, but that's not quite true. I think that for every album that's ever come out of Queen, we really picked the best of the batch. I'm not trying to hog a Queen album in any way. I have to make sure that I come up with good songs, and they looked upon me as the chief song writer, or Brian and I as the principal writers, but in a funny way that makes them write better songs. That doesn't mean I write the best songs, because the songs are hits, it just means that they come up with very good songs too.

I seem to participate more on Roger or John's tracks, as they let me help them and suggest things. Whereas Brian's got his own writing ideas and they're very strong, so I don't seem to be able to get into his ideas so much. With John and Roger's songs I sort of get in there at quite an early stage and they don't mind me tearing things apart and piecing it back together again. Sometimes I even take the whole song over, like with... and I don't mind saying it, with Roger's *Radio Ga Ga*. I instantly felt that there was going to be something one could build into a really good strong and saleable commodity there. And so he went on a skiing holiday for a week and I worked on it. But it's basically his song. He had the ideas all together and I just felt that there were some construction elements that were wrong. He just said, "Ok, you do what you want."

There's no way of telling how much a song is going to change until you're in the studio. A lot expands while you're actually in the recording process, like with *Somebody To Love* [1976]. I knew that I wanted a gospel choir feel to it, and I knew we'd have to do it all ourselves. That song is something like 160-piece choir effect. You can imagine how long it took to do – over and over and over again. We spent a week on that, but it was worth it. I never want to look back on one of our albums and think, "If only we'd spent longer, and done that, it would have been better!" We are perfectionists about things and we think it's worth spending that time. People probably think, "Oh God, they're in the studio again for four and a half months," but we think it's necessary because it just has to be right, that's all.

The phrase 'over-produced' is too easily applied to Queen, but it's just not true. If you look at it intelligently, there are certain songs that need that kind of attention. If we want overkill, we can do that. But then again, take the song *You Take My Breath Away*, that certainly is out of the Queen idiom, because

I left it as just a vocal and piano song – it needed that kind of sparseness. And *The Millionaires Waltz* needed yet another kind of treatment.

In terms of writing, producing and arranging, we learnt from the very early days of Queen that we would actually do all that ourselves. We were very reticent to have anybody else infiltrate our territory. So we learnt to do it all ourselves and keep it within the four of us. And that's the only way I know how to do it.

I think our lyrics have changed from the early days. I'm writing softer stuff at the moment. I'm at the stage where I like to write with simplicity and that means the song's structure as well as the lyrics. I got away from all that *Bohemian Rhapsody* stuff, and the *Killer Queen* lyrics. That was just a phase I was going through then [1974/75].

I think the people who buy our records now are interested in the change in Queen. They are used to us coming up with something different every time, so they adapt to that. I think sometimes they would be disappointed if we didn't do that. I never like to repeat the same formula more than once because I find it boring. I'm always looking for something different which is good because that's a challenge. That's something that comes naturally. The songs are diverse. We change with moods, we are adaptable. A lot of it is spontaneous, we don't really think about it too hard. I think that's the best way. If it's too planned then it would be too wooden and it wouldn't be us.

Chapter five: part 3

QUEEN SONGS

"We are all strong believers in doing things which are unusual,
not expected of us, and out of the ordinary.
We never want to get into a rut or become stale as a band,
and there is a danger of doing that when you have
been together as long as we have. There is a danger
of resting on your laurels and just getting lax, and there is no way
any of us would want that. We never want to stay still."

QUEEN (1973)
Keep Yourself Alive was a very good way of telling people what Queen was
about in those days.

QUEEN II (1974)
There was no deep meaning or concept in the album. At the time of recording
we conceived it impulsively. I wrote a song, *The March Of The Black Queen*,
for the album and that's when we got the idea of having white and black sides
– reflecting white and black moods. It became a good contrast.

Seven Seas Of Rhye is really just fictitious. I know it's like bowing out, or
the easy way out, but that's what it is. It was just a figment of my imagination.
At that time I was learning about a lot of things in song writing, like song
structure – I was just learning different techniques all the time.

On *Ogre Battle* we used a huge gong. It was even bigger than the one Pink
Floyd used on stage, and it took all Roger's strength to just lift the hammer!

The 'No Synths' thing* we put on as a joke, at first, and because we were frustrated, but it turned out to be quite a good idea, because we even managed to fool John Peel at the time. He said something in a review once about there being good use of Moog synthesizer, and actually it was just multi-tracked guitar.

SHEER HEART ATTACK (1974)

Killer Queen is about a high-class call girl. I was trying to say that classy people can be whores as well. That's what the song is about, though I'd prefer people to put their own interpretation upon it – to read what they like into it. People are used to hard rock energy music from Queen, yet with that single you almost expect Noel Coward to sing it. It's one of those bowler hat, black suspender numbers – not that Noel Coward would wear that.

We're very proud of that number. It's just one of the tracks I wrote for the album, it wasn't written as a single. I just wrote a batch of songs for *Sheer Heart Attack* and when I finished writing it, and when we recorded it, we found it was a very strong single. It really was. At that time it was very unlike Queen. It was another risk we took, but you know every risk we took, up to that time, paid off.

Killer Queen was another one I wrote the words for first. It was one song that was really out of the format that I usually write in. Generally the music comes first, but that time it was the words, along with the sophisticated style that I wanted to put across. A lot of my songs are fantasy, I can dream up all kinds of things.

Now I'm Here. That was nice. That was a Brian May thing. We released it after *Killer Queen*. It's a total contrast. It was just to show people that we can still do rock'n'roll – that we haven't forgotten our rock'n'roll roots. It's nice to do on stage. I enjoyed doing that live.

A NIGHT AT THE OPERA (1975)

A Night At The Opera is easily one of Queen's best. It took the longest to record out of all the first four albums. We didn't really cater for that, we just set upon it and said that we were going to do so many things. It took us about

* Queen included a 'No Synths' note on the inner sleeves of their early albums because they were fed up with journalists writing in error about their use of synthesizers.

four months to record and we nearly went over the deadline, with a tour approaching at the time. It was important to get the album the way we wanted it, especially after we've spent so long on it. Each song on *Opera* can stand up in its own right.

There were a lot of things we wanted to do on *Queen II* and *Sheer Heart Attack*, but there wasn't space enough. With *Opera* there was. Guitar-wise and with vocals we did things we've never done before. It featured every sound, from a tuba to a comb. Nothing was out of bounds.

There were just so many songs and styles we wanted to do. It makes a change to have short numbers as well a long ones. It's so varied that we were able to go to extremes. Every molecule on that album is us, just the four of us – every iota. There were no session men; not for strings, not for anything.

We produced the album in co-operation with Roy [Thomas] Baker, who'd had some amazing all-round experience and was a great help to us.

It may have been an expensive album – I think it cost us about £15,000 to £20,000, because we were determined to make it the best we possibly could, and I suppose we really wanted to prove we could do it – but the relief of getting it finished... I can't tell you!

Now then... *Death On Two Legs* was the most vicious lyric I ever wrote. It was so vindictive that Brian felt bad singing it. No-one would ever believe how much hate and venom went into the singing of that song, let alone the lyrics themselves. Just listen to the words carefully kiddies. It's a nasty little number which brings out my evil streak.

I don't usually like to explain what I was thinking when I wrote that song. It's about a nasty old man that I used to know. The words came very easy to me.

I decided that if I wanted to stress something strongly, like that, I might as well go the whole hog and not compromise. I had a tough time trying to get the lyrics across. I wanted to make them as coarse as possible. My throat was bleeding – the whole bit. I was changing lyrics every day trying to get it as vicious as possible. When the others first heard it they were in a state of shock. When I was describing it, they went, "Oh yeah!" but then they saw the words and they were frightened by it. But for me the step had been taken and I was completely engrossed in it, swimming in it. I was a demon for a few days.

The album needed a strong opening and what better way than to have the first words, 'You suck my blood like a leech'? Initially it was going to have the intro, and then everything stop, and the words, 'You, suck, my ****' – but that was going too far.

Let's just say that the song has made its mark!

Lazing On A Sunday Afternoon is a short track, just one minute and six seconds. It's a very perky spicy number, dears. Brian likes that one.

That's the way the mood takes me, you see. That's just one aspect of me – I can really change. Everything on *Sunday Afternoon* is something a bit different to the norm. I love doing the vaudeville side of things. It's quite a test. I love writing things like that and I'm sure I'm going to do more of that. It's a challenge too.

Then there's *Good Company*, written by Brian, a George Formby track with saxophones, trombone and clarinet – all sounds from Brian's guitar. We don't believe in having any session men, we do everything ourselves, from the high falsetto to the low bassy parts. It's all us.

It's a sign of transition. We could probably have done them on the first album, but you can't have it all, and it took until that fourth album to try to put it across. There are so many things we wanted to delve into. I always wanted to write something like that. *Ogre Battle* was written on a guitar, but then I got more into *Love Of My Life* and *Lily Of The Valley*-type things, on piano. I've always listened to that kind of music.

Seaside Rendezvous has a 1920's feel to it, and Roger does a tuba and clarinet thing on there too, vocally, if you see what I mean. I'm going to make him tap-dance too. I'll have to buy him some Ginger Rogers tap-shoes.

'39 was a little spacey number by Brian, a skiffle style of piece, which we'd never tried before. It's something that we have in us and people can't believe it. They can't believe it's us. It's something Brian May wanted to do and it's very, very unlike Queen, really. I think it's going to the B-side of *You're My Best Friend*.

Brian has an outrageously mammoth epic track, *The Prophet's Song*, which is one of our heaviest numbers to date. He's got his guitar extravaganza on it. You see, Brian's guitar is specially built, so he can almost make it speak. It will *talk* on this track.

The *Rhapsody* single took bloody ages, and *The Prophet's Song* alone took three weeks, but we had all the freedom we wanted and we were able to go to greater extremes. Fancy doing opera, for a start! I believe that album combined the outrageousness of *Queen II* with the good songs on *Sheer Heart Attack*. They are the finest songs ever written dears!

I'm In Love With My Car, the B-side of *Rhapsody*, was Roger's first hit. He wanted that very badly and I think he deserved it. It was a big hit in Europe.

Love Of My Life is a lovely little ballad. My classical influence comes into that. Brian plays real life-size harp on that. I remember thinking, "I'm going to force him to play until his fingers drop off!"

It's been adapted now on stage for guitar, but it was written on the piano. Everywhere we've been in the world, they know how to sing *Love Of My Life* – it's amazing to watch with so many people.

I once dedicated *Love Of My Life* to Kenny Everett, dears, on his radio programme [1976], for being so nice to us, and letting us infiltrate his 'Be Bop Bonanza' programme. It's from our *Sheer Heart Attack* album... Oh no, it's *A Night At The Opera*. God! We've made so many, I keep forgetting.

You're My Best Friend is John Deacon's song. I was very pleased with that, actually. John really started coming into his own at that time. He worked very hard at that, and it's very good, isn't it? It's very nice. It added to the versatility of Queen – do you know what I mean?

A DAY AT THE RACES (1976)
On *You Take My Breath Away* I multi-tracked myself. The others weren't used on that, for the voices. I played piano and that was basically it. I don't know how we managed to keep it that simple, you know, with all our overdubs and things. People seem to think that we're over complex, and it's not true. It depends on the individual track. If it needs it, we do it. So that track is pretty sparse actually, by Queen standards.

Long Away is a twelve-string thing written by Brian. It has very interesting harmonies.

For *Somebody To Love* we had the same three people singing on the big choir section, but I think it had a different kind of technical approach because it was a gospel way of singing – which was different to us. That track was me going a bit mad. I just wanted to write something in the Aretha Franklin kind of mode. I was inspired by the gospel approach she had on her earlier albums. Although it might sound like the same approach on the harmonies, it is very different in the studio because it's a different range.

The Millionaire Waltz is quite outlandish, really. It's the kind of track I like to put on every album – something way outside Queen's format. Brian orchestrated it fully with guitars, like he'd never done before. He went from tubas to piccolos to cellos. It took weeks. Brian's very finicky. That track is something that Queen had never undertaken before – a Strauss waltz.

It's all about John Reid, actually – our manager at the time. Again, I think I went a bid mad on that one. But it turned out alright I think – and it makes people laugh sometimes.

Actually I'd like to say that Brian did a very good job on the guitars. He really took his guitar orchestration to its limits. I don't know how he's ever going to out-do that one. And John played very nice bass on that. I think it's very good and we were patting ourselves on the back with that one. I really think it worked out well especially from the orchestration point of view. Brian has really used his guitar in a different sort of way. I know he's done lots of orchestrations before, but even so... very nice.

You And I – on the end of side one – is a track by John Deacon, his contribution to that album. His songs are getting better all the time. I'm getting a bit worried actually.

Tie Your Mother Down is one of Brian's heavies. In fact, I remember we played it at Hyde Park, at our picnic by the Serpentine, in the summer of 1976, before we had actually recorded it. I was able to come to grips with the song in front of a live audience before I had to record the vocal in the studio. Being a very raucous track, it worked well for me.

That song has really done us proud, especially in England. It's been a very, very strong live track. And I think it sounds good. It's opened up a lot of new areas.

White Man, the B side of *Somebody To Love* is Brian's song too. It's a very bluesy track and it gave me the opportunity to do raucous vocals. I think it'll be a great stage number.

Good Old Fashioned Lover Boy is another one of my vaudeville numbers. I always do a vaudeville track, though *Lover Boy* is more straightforward than *Seaside Rendezvous*, for instance. It's quite simple piano/vocals with a catchy beat; the album needs it to sort of ease off.

Drowse is a very interesting song of Roger's. Roger is very rock'n'roll. It's got great slide guitar from Brian, and Roger's done octave vocals. It's a very hummable tune, actually. I sing it all the time.

The album – *A Day At The Races*, not *Horse Feathers*, which was another film by the Marx Brothers – ends with a Japanese thing, a track from Brian called *Teo Torriatte*, which means 'let us cling together.' It's a very emotional track, one of his best. Brian plays harmonium and some lovely guitar. It's a nice song to close the album.

NEWS OF THE WORLD (1977)

We Are The Champions was the most egotistical and arrogant song I've ever written. I was thinking about football when I wrote it. I wanted a participation song, something the fans could latch on to. It was aimed at the masses. I thought we'd see how they took it. It worked a treat. When we performed it at a private concert in London, the fans actually broke into a football chant between numbers. Of course, I've given it more theatrical subtlety than an ordinary football chant. You know me!

I certainly wasn't thinking about the press when I wrote it. I never think about the British music press these days. It was really meant to be offered to the musicians, as well as the fans. I suppose it could also be construed as my version of *I Did It My Way*. We have made it, and it certainly wasn't easy. No bed of roses as the song says. And it's still not easy. That song was taken up by football fans because it's a winner's song. I can't believe that someone hasn't written a new song to overtake it.

Spread Your Wings is very John Deacon – but with more raucous guitars. After I'd done the vocals, John put all these guitars in, and the mood has changed. I think it's his strongest song to date.

THE GAME (1980)

I wrote *Crazy Little Thing Called Love* on guitar and played rhythm on the record, and it works really well because Brian gets to play all those lead guitar fills as well as his usual solo. I'm somewhat limited by the number of chords I know. I'm really just learning, but I hope to play more guitar in the future. That song is not typical of my work, but that's because nothing is typical of my work.

Another One Bites The Dust was a dance hit, but it doesn't mean we're going to do everything in that style from this point on. We like to experiment, although I have learnt a lot from all this black rhythm disco music, from Michael Jackson, Stevie Wonder and Aretha Franklin.

75

UNDER PRESSURE (collaboration with David Bowie, 1981)
Under Pressure came about by pure chance, my dears. David came in to see us one day in the recording studios we owned at the time, in Montreux, where we were working. We began to dabble on something together, and it happened very spontaneously and very quickly indeed. We were both overjoyed by the result.

It may have been a totally unexpected thing, but as a group we are all strong believers in doing things which are unusual, not expected of us, and out of the ordinary. We never want to get into a rut or become stale as a band, and there is a danger of doing that when you have been together as long as we have. There is a danger of resting on your laurels and just getting lax, and there is no way any of us would want that.

David was a real pleasure to work with. He is a remarkable talent. When I saw him play in the stage version of 'The Elephant Man' on Broadway, his performance fuelled me with thoughts about acting. It is something I may do in the future, but right now I'm looking at other projects to do with Queen. We never want to stay still. There are so many vistas still to explore.

THE WORKS (1984)
I wrote a song with Brian for this album. There should be an eclipse!

It's called *Is This The World We Created*. I like the way we approached that song. We were looking at all the songs we had on the album and we thought that the one thing we didn't have was one of those real limpid ballads – or the lilting type; the *Love Of My Life*-type things. And rather than one of us going back and thinking of one, I just said to Brian, "Why don't we just think of something right here," and that song just evolved in about two days. He got an acoustic guitar and I just sat next to him and we worked it out together.

If we actually thought beforehand that we should sit down and write a song together, I don't think it would ever have happened, because then all kinds of things, like egos, play havoc, and who does what. But this way, we didn't have time to think about it. We just went in there and got it together. If it didn't work we were going to throw it out, but it seemed to work and it was quite strong, so we said yes, this should work as a tail out of the album. And later we did it at Live Aid.

THE MIRACLE (1989)
Personally, I don't like titles which give an album a concept, as it sometimes gives the wrong image. For example, the working title of *The Miracle* album was *The Invisible Man*. There's a song on it with the same title, and we talked about making a video and doing some magical things in it. But you can imagine that the journalists will have taken the title in the wrong sense. Anyway the title was *The Invisible Man* until the very last week. I think it was Roger who started to say, "Come on, this title won't do!" So we thought about changing it, and there was a song called *The Miracle*, so we thought that would express ourselves well. So we made the title *The Miracle*. Of course, lots of people will have thought that we think of our work as miracles, but huh! If they want to think like that, they can. It basically just came from the title of one song on the album.

It was okay, but we had our various fisticuffs.

INNUENDO (1991)
I'm pleased with my vocals on this album. *Innuendo* is a word I often use in Scrabble. For Queen, it's a perfect title.

Chapter six

I'M LONELY BUT NO-ONE CAN TELL

*"If I wanted children I'd just go to Harrods and buy one. They
sell anything there. Buy two, and you get a nanny thrown in!"*

When I have a relationship it is never a half-hearted one. I don't believe in half
measures or compromise. I just can't bear to compromise about anything. I
give everything I've got because that's the way I am.

I try to hold back when I'm attracted to someone but I just can't control
love. It runs riot. I fall in love far too quickly and end up getting hurt all the
time. Maybe I just draw the wrong kind of people to me? I've got scars all
over. But I can't help myself because basically I'm a softie.

In terms of love, you're never in control and I hate that feeling. I've cried
rivers. I may be hard on the exterior, but I'm very soft-centred. I have this
hard, macho shell which I project on stage but there's a much softer side
too, which melts like butter. I'm a true romantic, just like Rudolph Valentino,
but some articles make me sound so damned cold.

I have a soft side and a hard side, with not a lot in between. If the right
person finds me I can be very vulnerable, a real baby, which is invariably
when I get trodden on, but sometimes I'm hard, and when I'm strong no
one can get to me. Now and again the quills come out – and they're sharp!

I'm a very dominant person in my relationships. I'm also a very possessive
person. I can go to great lengths trying to be loyal just to prove a point, but

the moment I find someone has betrayed me, I go the other way. Betrayed, I'm an ogre!

I'm a man of extremes and that can be very destructive. I can be very over-emotional and that can be a very destructive trait in me too. I seem to eat people up when they get too close and destroy them, no matter how hard I try to make things work. There must be a destructive element in me because I try very hard to build up relationships but somehow I drive people away. They always blame the end of the love affair on me because I'm the successful one. Who ever I'm with they seem to get into a battle of trying to match up to me, and over-compensating.

I spoil my lovers terribly. I like to make them happy and I get so much pleasure out of giving them wonderful, expensive presents, but then they end up treading all over me. When I lay myself bare on the floor it just seems to be my downfall.

Sometimes I wake up in a cold sweat, in fear because I'm alone. That's why I go out looking for someone who will love me, even if it's just for a one night stand. My one night stands are just me playing my part. What I really like is a lot of loving. I fall in love and then I end up getting hurt and scarred. It seems I just can't win.

In one way I think the more mishaps I have, the better the songs I write are going to be. Once I find somebody, find a long-lasting relationship, bang goes all the research for wonderful songs! I'm sort of living on past mishaps. Well, having said all of that, I don't know… I don't know what's in store for me. I want a challenge. I always want it that way. I think my system is just conditioned to that. The moment it gets too nice, I become bored. I spoil it for myself.

Yes I'm gay. I've done all that. I'm as gay as a daffodil, dears. But I couldn't fall in love with a man the way I could with a girl. I don't go out to have very gay company, but in this business it's very hard to find loyal friends and keep them. Among my friends are a lot of gay people and a lot of girls – and a lot of *old* men too! I move in a theatrical world and people can draw their own connotations from that. I had a girlfriend I lived with for five years – Mary. I had boyfriends as well. It would destroy all the mystery if I always explained everything about myself. To actually come out with it and go into huge detail about all those things, to be honest, is a bit beneath me. I have maybe a wider sexual taste than most people, but that's as far as I'm going to go.

I'm a human being. I'd like people to recognise the fact that I'm a human being. It's like I'm handicapped, because people immediately go for my so-called stage persona. No-one loves the real me. Inside, they're all in love with my fame and stardom. Therefore I have to virtually fight. Most of the time it works against me. I want a relationship, but I feel I have to fight that all the time. It's like I created a monster. I have to find somebody to accept that, in terms of a relationship, but it's very hard. You try to segregate the two and it's not easy – it's like two sides of a coin. There have been romances in my life that have gone wrong and it is very hard to find someone genuine. You can't tell whether they want you or Freddie Mercury the pop star... and *He's* someone quite different!

I can be a good lover, but I think after all these years I'm not a very good partner for anybody. I've had a lot of lovers, of course. I've had more lovers than Liz Taylor! Both male and female. I've tried relationships on either side, but my affairs never seem to last. All of them went wrong. Obviously I'm not a good catalyst. Love is Russian roulette for me.

Finding that wonderful person is very hard and sometimes I try too hard. I was running away with myself. I mean, the more I was upset with the relationship, the more there was a backlog of stress and hardship and those things. Oh dear! It sounds like this could be like a real sob story, but I don't mean it that way. I feel I'm walking around with scars all over the place and I just think I couldn't take another scar.

I get hurt, but I try not to make too much of a show of it. I'm not a person to hold a grudge. At the actual moment of a betrayal it's like a knife in your back, and of course my initial reaction is, "I'm gonna get that fucker!" But it does fade. I will myself into that kind of thing. I just let it go. It's not worth it. I've been let down many times, but I just grit my teeth, bite my tongue and say, "Fuck 'em!"

In many cases we end up being friends, after a while, which is quite amazing for me. There are so many people who have fucked me up, basically, and I think, "Never again." And some of my close friends say, "How could you just overlook that?" You see, I'm a softie... I'm a peach.

I'm possessed by love! Isn't everybody? Most of my songs are love ballads and things to do with sadness and torture and pain. I seem to write a lot of sad songs because I'm a very tragic person. But there is always an element of humour at the end.

I once wrote a song called *My Love Is Dangerous* [1985]. I feel that maybe that's what my love is – dangerous. I haven't actually analysed myself, but after all these years I just feel I'm not a very good partner for anybody, and I think that's what my love is. My love is dangerous. Who wants their love to be safe anyway? Can you imagine writing a song called 'My Love Is Safe'? It would never sell.

I generate a lot of friction, so I'm not the easiest person to have a relationship with. I'm the nicest person you could meet, my dears, but I'm very hard to live with. I don't think anyone could put up with me, and I think sometimes I try too hard. In one way I am greedy, I just want it all my own way, but doesn't everybody? I'm a very loving person, you know, and I'm a very giving person. I demand a lot, but I do give a lot in return.

I also found that in a way, over the years, I've become bitter. I just don't trust anybody because I've been let down so many times. The more you've been let down, the more hurt you endure. I find it very hard to open up to people because I just don't trust the buggers. You just can't win in my situation, and that's the way it is.

When you have success it becomes very difficult. You find out the real baddies. I just take it as it comes. In fact, that's why I've built up a very hard exterior. I mean most of the time when people talk to me, I immediately think,

"What do they want? Is he after this or that?" So it's very hard for people to get to know me. I have to go through a big sort of sifting process. I have to weed them out. I probably might do it to the wrong person sometimes, but I have to do that. You don't welcome people with open arms all the time – you just have to vet them.

Success has brought me millions of pounds, and worldwide adulation, but not the thing we all need – a loving relationship. You can be loved by so many thousands of people, yet still be the most loneliest person. And the frustration of that makes it even worse, because it's hard for people to understand that you can be lonely.

Most people wonder how someone like Freddie Mercury can be lonely? He has money, he has cars and chauffeurs, he has the lot. You can seem to have everything, and yet have nothing. Maybe one day I'll catch up with myself and that will be my downfall. In fact, sometimes that kind of loneliness is the hardest to bear because within all that, all the people around you, you're still lonely. You see, loneliness doesn't just mean shut off in a room by yourself, it can be that you're in a crowded area but still be the most lonely person, and that's the most hurtful thing.

This sounds like 'Poor, Lonely, Freddie.' I'll be inundated with offers!

It's difficult for people in my position. The slightest thing can turn it all back. Sometimes you can be a very strong person and you can build things up, against all odds, and it takes one tiny little thing, and that little four letter word can send you cart-wheeling back. But you can still strive for it. I've tried, but it's always gone wrong. It's so much heartache and I just don't want any more of that. I really don't. I think love always comes first, but love can let you down. You have to be so damn strong. Love can ruin everything that you've built up, if you let it. I suppose you have to be a hard-faced bitch.

A lot of the people that the media build up to be so strong, are not that at all underneath. Sometimes the strongest people can suddenly just collapse. It's like you've blown up a balloon and one prick can make it go, whoosh! You have to be very careful.

I live life to the full. My sex drive is enormous. I sleep with men, women, cats – you name it. I'll go to bed with anything! My bed is so huge it can comfortably sleep six. I prefer my sex without any involvement and there were times when I was extremely promiscuous. I used to be just an old slag who got up every morning, scratched his head, and wondered who he wanted to fuck today. I just lived for sex. I'm a very sexual person but I'm much more choosy now than I used to be. I want to have my cake and eat it too. I want my security but I also want my freedom.

At the moment I'm living totally alone, believe it or not, and I'm loving it. I've got rid of three people that worked with me and that was wonderful. I was so scared of doing that because I thought I was going to hurt them, but then I thought, "No, just do it." So there you are. They've gone. Before, I thought I couldn't live alone, there had to be people around, but now I find I can do that and it's fine.

I have nobody staying with me at the moment. I have a cleaning lady that comes in – who sometimes breaks the odd treasured ornament… if she'd been around in Louis XIV time, there wouldn't be any antiques left today - and Mary comes in too and looks after me. It sounds poverty stricken, doesn't it? But I love it. I love the space. I've finally created some sort of space for myself. It's this feeling of being free – not that I was ever bogged down.

If you listen to my song *Living On My Own,* that is very me. It's living on my own, but having fun. There's a bit in the middle where I do my scat singing and I'm just saying that when you think about somebody like me, my lifestyle, I have to go around the world and live in hotels and that can be a very lonely life. But I chose it. That song is not dealing with people who are living on their own in basement flats, or situations like that, it's *my* living on my own. I mean, you can have a whole shoal of people looking after you, but in the end they all go away and you are in a hotel room on your own. I'm not complaining though. It's a different kind of living on my own. People with my success can be lonely and can live on their own as well. I'm just saying that I'm living on my own and I'm having a boogie time! Does that make sense, honey?

Anyway, you can't revel in the success and then wake up one morning and say, "No, I don't want to be a superstar today. I want to go out in the streets on my own." It's impossible. When you're a celebrity it's hard to approach somebody and say, "Look, I'm normal underneath."

I'm very content at the moment, in terms of happiness, and in terms of love. It's something that I had to come to terms with, which is completely new to me. You always think that is the goal, and I want to strive for that. Suddenly I feel this is where I am, and the object is to make the best of it.

You have your ideals in terms of love, and I always thought it would be this way or that way. I've tried and tried, and I've failed. I can't categorise it. I've learned to come to grips with it. This is a form of happiness where I have to lump it or leave it. I think I'm honestly quite content now. And rather than not be content and keep gnawing and clawing at it, which is not going work, I go home and lock that door and just carry on.

I would have loved to have found a really beautiful relationship with somebody, a long-lasting one-to-one, but I don't feel I'm going to get that in my life now and I don't think my life can actually cater for it. It never seemed to work out. This is what I think my life is going to be, and I have to come to terms with it. If you tell yourself that, you can let off steam and say, "Fuck it! It's not going to happen that way so don't get so tangled up about it."

I love being free. I want to be free as a bird. I think I've gotten too used to it. To be honest I feel like I'm having such a good time right now, that I'm going to keep on doing it. But... you never know! Like Elton – I think we're the same age, we average 40 – people change, and suddenly you want to settle down and have babies, just like he did. I think he just got there a bit quicker than expected. I thought he would have waited, but you never know, it could happen.

I really can't see myself being married. No-one would marry me, dears... the dowry was too high. And if I wanted children I'd just go to Harrods and buy one. They sell anything there. Yes, that will do! I'll go to Harrods and buy one. Buy two, and you get a nanny thrown in!

Nobody wants to share their life with me. It's like old Hollywood stories where those wonderful actresses couldn't carry on a relationship because their careers came first. That's the way it is with me. I can't stop the wheel for a second and devote myself to a love affair because all sorts of business problems would pile up. The wheel has to keep turning and that makes it very hard for anyone to live with me and be happy. It's just the rigors of success I guess.

I wouldn't sacrifice my career if a partner wanted me to. It's my career that keeps me going. What else would I do? Dig weeds, get fat and be beautifully in love? No, I'd like to remain as successful as I am, write beautiful songs *and* be in love – not that it's worked up 'til now. My private life will always be erratic. I'll keep on trying.

I'm not married to music, I'm married to love. I may not have time for it, but I'm not married to it. Music is my work, it's my job. It may not be 9-5, but it's my job. I see music as something that I earn my living at. I'm a total romantic and I'm married to love and people.

In 1984 Freddie met Jim Hutton. They would remain together as a couple until Freddie's death in November 1991.

I wanted a kind of genuine tranquillity after the storm. Everybody expects me to have stormy relationships. I was virtually living my own media thing, as it were, where you get caught up in it, and I thought that was the way I should be. I always thought I had to be the spokesman, the captain of the ship. I was working so hard, performing for everybody, even off-stage, and then I just thought, "No, you don't have to do it. Let others do it. Just be yourself and try and be run-of-the-mill." I thought that I had to perform, I had to take over the show and everything, wherever I was. And then I just thought, "No, you don't have to do that. Let them tell you you're boring." And it's wonderful. So people might say, "Oh my God you're boring. You're not saying a thing," but I love it now. I say, if I'm boring, then amuse yourself by finding something else to do. You see, they relied on me to entertain them. Once, if somebody said I'm boring, I would go mad, I'd have had a flap... but now I love it.

I just thought, "Look, discard all that and start afresh. Try to think of yourself as somebody different." You can't do it in patches.

I'm very happy with my relationship at the moment and I honestly couldn't ask for better. It's a kind of... solace. Yes that's a good word. We won't call it menopause! There is this kind of solace that I've got now. I don't have to try so hard. I don't have to prove myself now. I've got a very understanding relationship. It sounds so boring, but it's wonderful.

I've finally found that niche I was looking for all my life, and no fucker in this universe is going to upset it.

Chapter seven

LOVE OF MY LIFE

"I'd love to have a baby, yes.
But I'd rather have another cat."

Mary is one of my closest friends in the world. Ours is a pure friendship and a friendship of the highest standard. It's an instinctive thing. I have built up an immense bond with Mary. I open up to her more than anybody else. We have gone through a lot of ups and downs in our time together, but that has made our relationship all the stronger. I know a lot of people find it hard to understand our relationship. Other people who come into our lives just have to accept it. We love each other very much and look after each other. I don't want anybody else.

All my lovers asked me why they couldn't replace Mary, but it's simply impossible. Mary is my common-law wife. To me, it *was* a marriage. What is marriage anyway, something that you sign? As far as we were concerned, we *were* married and we carry on now like we are. Marriage is a term for *other* people. You can actually go through the entire process without saying you're married. Just because a piece of paper ties you… I don't know about that. It's farcical.

I treat Mary as my common-law wife and we're getting on fine. It's where the heart is that matters. We're happy with each other and it doesn't matter what other people think. We believe in each other and that's enough for me. We believe in each other, so fuck everybody else. Nobody should tell us what to do. As far as I'm concerned we are married. It's a God given situation.

I met Mary around 1970 and ever since then we have had a wonderful relationship. I met her at the Biba boutique in London, where she worked. I was a Biba freak right from the beginning, way before it got turned into a big department store. When I used to go there it was just a small boutique.

We were closer than anybody else, though we stopped living together after about seven years. Our love affair ended in tears, but a deep bond grew out of it, and that's something nobody can take away from us. It's unreachable. People always ask me about sexuality and all those things, right from the early days, but I couldn't fall in love with a man the same way as I have with Mary.

I'm not built to be a family man. I'm much too restless and highly strung for that. Mary and I have a good understanding. She gives me the freedom I need. I don't feel jealous of her lovers because, of course, she has a life to lead, and so do I. Basically, I try to make sure she's happy with whoever she's with, and she tries to do the same for me. We look after each other and that's a wonderful form of love.

Over the years I have become bitter and I don't trust anybody else because they have let me down so many times. I just don't trust anybody now. The higher up you go on the ladder or the more friends you make or the more successful you become, it seems to be that you trust less people rather than the other way round. I find it hard. I find it harder and harder to trust people. I sometimes think, "Oh, this person's going to be okay," and then I find I come a cropper. To be honest I can only name one really dear person who I can actually open up to and feel really happy with. The others, I have to think twice about. I'm cautious. Maybe I'm getting a bit too cautious, but that's the way it is.

Sometimes a good friend is much more valuable than a lover. Apart from Mary I don't have any real friends. I don't think I do. Friends come and go. A real *true* friend for me has to be very strong to put up with me. I think Mary has gone through just about everything with me. She has the depth and the qualities to adapt to me and talk to me about very serious things. Even if we are not together at the time, I talk to her a lot on the phone. She's about the only person I can think of. Otherwise I just fend for myself and I cross my hurdles in my own way.

Finding a few very close people, that would be enough for me, but trying to get really true friends in this business is very hard. People tell me they're my friends, but I'm never certain. Sometimes when they get too close I think they seem to destroy me. I don't know, maybe it's my nature. I've said this before, but when they get too close they seem to tread all over me. If I lay myself bare I seem to get trampled on. At this point in time I seem to make fewer and fewer friends, but life goes on.

I'd love to have a baby, yes. That would be nice, but it will never happen. I'd rather have another cat. Maybe in another couple of years or in another three years time I might have a settled down feeling, but at this moment in time, no, I'm going through a phase where I want to rest. For the first time in my life I've become very content. I want to see how far it goes and *then* I can think of things like that.

I have built up this immense bond with Mary and it seems to grow and grow. If I go first I'm going to leave everything to her. Nobody else gets a penny – except my cats. They deserve it. I had four cats, but one passed away – poor fucking thing! She had to be put to sleep.

There have been only two individuals who have given back as much love to me as I gave to them: Mary, with whom I had a long affair, and our cat, Jerry.

I might have all the problems in the world, but I have Mary and that gets me through. She only lives about two minutes from me. I still see her every day and I am as fond of her now as I have ever been. I'll love her until I draw my last breath. We'll probably grow old together.

Chapter eight

I'M JUST A SINGER WITH A SONG

*"It was like painting a picture – where you have to step away from
it to see what it's like. I was stepping away from Queen and
I think it gave everybody a shot in the arm."*

In the early days when Queen was formed a lot of people were asking, "When
are you going to do your solo project?" But the funny thing is, Brian did a
solo project [1983] and Roger did two [1981/1984]. I was virtually the last
one to do it. To be honest I thought we would all be doing solo albums long
before we did. I suppose when we made a Queen album they were like four
solo projects within themselves. I had my bunch of songs and Brian had his,
and Roger and John had theirs, so it was like four little solo projects working
side by side, and then we put them together.

I think every artist who's in a group wants to do a solo project sometime
or other. It's something in everyone's metabolism. I mean, I always wanted
to do it but I think most people thought I was going to record one in the
first five years, and then break up the band. But it wouldn't work that way
because there is an inbred jealousy, and they'd all wait to see if my album
did better than the last Queen album. That is a good challenge, in that if my
album did do very well, then we'd take the view that the next Queen album
would have to be even better still.

I was always keen to do a solo album. I just wanted it to be the right time
and the right place so that I could actually work properly on the songs that I
wanted to do before I got too old.

There was a time when we were doing tours extensively. We used to do American tours that lasted three or four months and towards the end it was terrible. I never wanted to go on stage ever again. If you're playing the same songs for three months, doing the same routine, you just need time away, but we would go into a studio and make an album, then tour the world, and then go back. That was the routine. We didn't have any time to break away and we virtually did that for eight or nine years. I was getting very bored and so were the others, and I needed to get away and do different things.

So, my *Mr Bad Guy* album was just a breather, a chance to do some things that I wanted to do without the others. But it certainly wasn't a split from Queen. It was just a form of outlet, something in me that I wanted to do. I wanted to write a batch of songs that actually came out under the name of Freddie Mercury and I wanted to do all the things I wasn't able to do within the band. In fact, some of the songs that were discarded from Queen albums ended up on my solo album, but they are good.

When you're doing solo projects you are your own boss, and I find that when I'm my own boss completely, it's easier for me. I make all the decisions and although that's harder sometimes, I can get things done quicker. You could call it an ego trip, you could call it going off on a tangent, you could call it anything, but it's basically just a batch of songs I wanted to do *my* way... I sound like Frank Sinatra.

I had a lot of ideas bursting to get out and there were a lot of musical territories I wanted to explore which I really couldn't do within Queen. I wanted to cover such things as reggae rhythms and I did a couple of tracks with an orchestra. The rest of the band encouraged me to do it. To be honest I would have preferred to have all of the band members play on it, but then it would not have been a Freddie Mercury solo album. If it was going to be a genuine solo album, they had to stay out of it, and that's all there is to it. I think they would have loved to have played on some of the tracks but then they would have become Queen tracks, so there was a certain amount of discipline I had to exercise.

Initially I had an idea that I wanted all kinds of famous people to appear on it. I had been working with Michael Jackson for a while [1982] and at the time he said he would appear on one of the tracks. But in the end it got too late because it's difficult to get these people to be at a certain time and place. So by the time I actually got into recording, I found I was doing it all, and it went the other way and I just decided I wanted to do it completely myself. Basically the musicians I used were German session players, who are very good in their own right but they're not as famous as Michael Jackson or Rod Stewart. I'm glad, though, because I think that it's the best way I could have come up with my first solo album.

I put my heart and soul into *Mr Bad Guy* and I think it's a very natural album. It had some very moving ballads – things to do with sadness and pain, but at the same time they were frivolous and tongue-in-cheek, because that's my nature. I think the songs on that album reflect the state of my life, a diverse selection of moods and a whole spectrum of what my life was.

As far as the title *Mr Bad Guy* is concerned, it is to do with me. *Mr Bad Guy* IS me. I won't explain that totally, you can take it from there.

There Must Be More To Life Than This is a song about people who are lonely. It's basically another love song, but it's hard to call it that because it encompasses other things too. It's all to do with why people get themselves into so many problems. It's mostly that, but I don't want to dwell on that too much. It's just one of those songs that I had for a while. Michael Jackson happened to hear it and liked it and if it had worked out we would have done it together, but I wanted it on this album, so I did it without his help. He's going to cry when he hears it!

Actually I liked all the songs on the album, but in the end one of my favourite tracks was *Love Me Like There's No Tomorrow* because of the way it came out. It was a very personal thing. I wrote it in five minutes and everything just gelled into place. It was just very emotional, very very strong. I love that track.

When I had finished the album I was lost for a title, but as far as I'm concerned album titles are immaterial. It's what you listen to that matters, not what the title is. Don't judge a book by its cover – although, there is a beautiful photograph of me on the cover. Originally I called the LP *Made In Heaven*, and then it changed. But I was not Made In Heaven... a lightning bolt didn't suddenly go Crack!

I was pleased with the album and I was also pleased with my voice. I like it husky. That's why I smoke – to get that husky voice. I dedicated this album to cat lovers everywhere. Screw everybody else!

Yes, I want it to be successful. It mattered to me a lot because I'd made a piece of music which I wanted to be accepted in the biggest way possible. People said that if it wasn't a hit I should sue Warner Brothers! But I wasn't worried that it might not be successful because if it wasn't, I would just go out and make another one.

When I was planning to do my second solo project I really didn't want it to be just another bunch of songs. I wanted it to have some kind of bearing, something different, to have another stamp to it that spear-headed the damn thing. It could be anything that made it different from another boring studio album. No matter how good my songs were, they'd just be another bunch of songs that you bung on a tape and release. So I was looking for ideas in that direction and suddenly these two wonderful names came up like a tidal wave, and they were Montserrat Caballé.

It really was a shot in the arm and all those clichés. It was something that wasn't calculated, it came rocketing out of the sky and just fell upon me. It virtually enveloped me and I could think of nothing else. It was fabulous. There was so much scope, so much life and energy in it, and as far as I'm concerned it wasn't just a work thing. I was totally in awe.

I think Montserrat has a marvellous voice, and on Spanish television I happened to mention it and she heard it. Next thing I knew she called me up and said, "Let's do something together." I was completely flabbergasted. Though I adored opera, I had never thought about singing it.

So, I flew off to Barcelona to meet her. I was really nervous. I wasn't sure how to behave or what I should say to her. Thankfully she made me feel very at ease right from the start and I realised that both of us had the same kind of humour. She said, "What's your favourite number?" I said, "Number one." Then she said, "From now on I call you my Number One," so I said, "I'll call you my Super Diva!" It was great. She jokes and she swears and she doesn't take herself too seriously. That really thrilled and surprised me because up until then I had been labouring under the illusion that all great opera singers were stern, aloof and quite intimidating. But Montserrat was wonderful. I told her I loved her singing and had her albums and asked if she'd heard of me. She told me she enjoyed listening to my music and had Queen albums in her collection, too. She even thought I might ask her to sing some rock and roll, but I said, "No, no, I'm not going to give you all those Brian May guitar parts to sing – that's the last thing I want to do!" She was very game to try it though.

I wasn't going to just approach her and talk it over with her, because I mean you just can't do those things. I thought I must bring to her a little idea of what she might be getting into, in terms of the music, because trying to explain things musically is so much harder. So I wrote a couple of pieces with Mike Moran, with her voice in mind, and I played her a couple of them, which she immediately took to, and that was how it started.

I thought we would only do one song, or a duet, but she said, "Only one song! You only want to do one?" And I said, "Let's see how we get on and if you like more of my music…" and then she asked, "How many songs does a normal rock'n'roll album have?" "Ten," I said. So she replies, "Well let's do ten songs then." I thought, "It's amazing. I'm going into opera. Forget rock'n'roll!"

I said that I'd write the songs and she would have to come in and try things out. So she looked up her schedule and said, "I have three days spare in May, and that's all." She thought she could just come in and do it like that – that's the way they work you see. I had to have it all prepared, but I knew three days was pushing it.

It's so ridiculous when you think about it, her and me together. But if we have something musically together, it doesn't matter what we look like or where we come from. When she said, "Let's make an album!" I thought, "My God, what am I going to do now?" because you just don't turn the Super Diva down. I thought I'd better put my money where my mouth is. I'm glad I did it because it was such a different thing to do. It was totally un-rock'n'roll, and something that really required a lot of discipline.

The last thing I wanted was a sort of forced combination, and she laid it on the line and just said, "Look, I'd love to do something. We're two musicians, and if it doesn't work out we'll say it's not working and call it a day." It was a real turning point, a proper turning point in my career, because she has taken to me in such a way that I just keep being floored by it. My God, I couldn't believe that somebody of her ilk and of her stature, and of her world, wanted to duet with me.

There was an added stress because it was a big risk. It was something that I don't think anybody else had done before. I had to do research to get some sort of operatic knowledge, to make sure that I was using her voice in the right way. So I spent a long time talking to her and listening to a lot of her records to find out her finer points, so that I could actually use them in the music. I wanted to hear what she could do and use the finest qualities in the songs that I was writing. I then had to see how my voice matched with hers. There's no point in just having a wonderful song and finding out that the two voices don't match or agree with each other, so you really have to work twice as hard. By meeting Montserrat I learned so much more about the music, and I have so much respect for it.

I had no operatic training at all and it's too late for me to start now, dears. I've never had any kind of formal training actually. It's just come through extensive singing all these years. I don't think rock'n'roll singers have any kind of training, their training is playing on the road. My voice has had enough beating, so it's a bit late to go and have any kind of training. I mean this is my voice and that's it. I just have a range which goes up and down depending on what mood I'm in. But that's the voice she wanted, she didn't want me to ape anybody, you see. She wanted my natural voice.

I think the music just ran away with itself, to be honest, and I was doing songs that I'd never done before, the sort of songs to suit our voices. I found it very difficult writing them and singing them because all the registers had to be right and they're all duets. I didn't know how the Queen fans would react to it. It is a bit of a... *thingy*! You can't put it under a label, can you? The worst thing they could call it is 'rock opera' – which is so boring.

With the *Barcelona* album I had a little bit more freedom and a bit of scope to actually try out some of my crazy ideas. Montserrat kept telling me that she found a new lease of life and a new found freedom. Those were her own words, and I was very taken by it. She told me on the phone that she loves the way our voices sound together... and I was smiling from my ass to my elbow, my dears. I sat at home like I'd just swallowed the canary, thinking, "Ooh! There's a lot of people who'd like to be in my shoes right now."

Montserrat has this amazing personality and it's quite spellbinding. She has this air of dominating a room. I've seen a lot of people like that; pop stars, or whatever you call them, actually trying so hard to go into a room and make sure they're noticed, but she just has this natural air and grace. The difference is really amazing, where she walks into a room and commands people's attention just by being so genuine that you can't help but be enveloped in it. That's how the opera people like to treat their divas. They're like goddesses.

She's like a dream, but at the same time I wasn't going to be all gushing, otherwise I wouldn't be able to do anything. The last thing she wanted was to be able to step all over me. She wanted a guiding force, as well, because she was singing my songs. I had to be strong in that way so I worked my ass off on that album. I worked until I dropped. But Montserrat was absolutely tremendous. Most of the recording was done around her schedule. I mean she just bulldozed around the world singing everywhere. She'll do an opera here, a recital there, with very little time in between. She has amazing energy, it was unbelievable. She ran me ragged my dears!

A Montserrat Caballé performance is sensational. She has that same kind of emotion as Aretha Franklin. The way she delivers a song is so very natural,

"To get some of the biggest stars in the world together at one event is quite a feat. Live Aid is going to be chaotic. Lots of friction, and we're all going to try and out-do each other. We're just going to go on there and play." Freddie came, he sang, he performed, and he conquered. As Brian May rightly noted, "It was Freddie's finest hour." July 13th 1985.

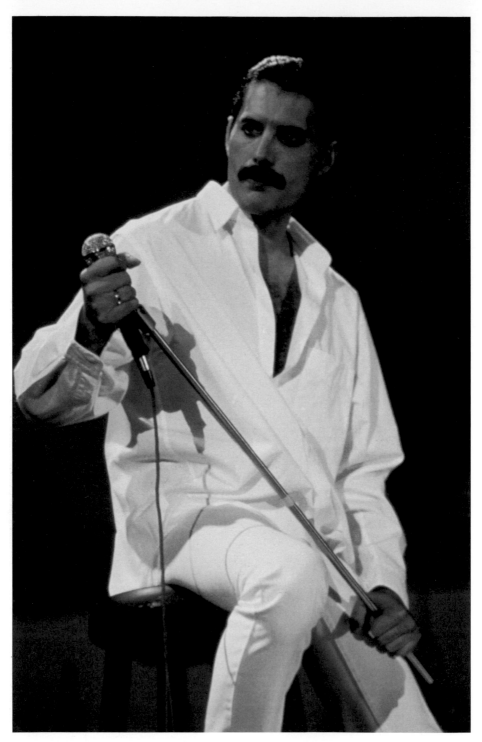

Many forget that Queen appeared not once, but twice at Live Aid. Having stolen the show earlier in the afternoon with a storming 20 minute medley of hits, Freddie returned to the stage with Brian May just before the finale to perform a moving recital of *Is This*

The World We Created, the song they wrote together.
Just look at all those hungry mouths we have to feed
Take a look at all the suffering we breed
So many lonely faces scattered all around
Searching for what they need

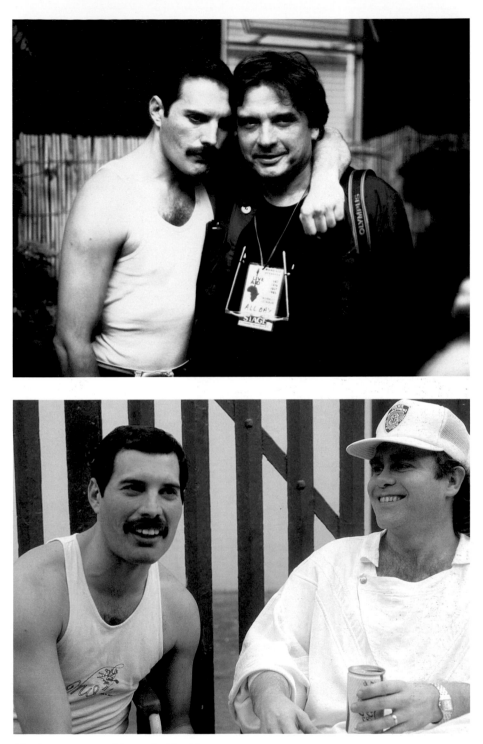

A lovely moment captured forever, Freddie with
photographer David Bailey backstage at Live Aid, and
with Elton John, at the same... two legends together!

Freddie and David Bowie confer
backstage at Live Aid, July 1985.

With Brian May in Budapest, during Queen's last tour in 1986. The two
are rehearsing the Hungarian folk song they will perform together – a
unique recital – at a concert at the Nepstadion on July 27th. Ultimately
Freddie sang the piece in Hungarian, reading from a note on his hand, and
the audience went wild. Queen's gesture was much appreciated.

A rare moment. At Musicland Studios, Munich,
Freddie gives another performance his ALL, as ever,
this time recording *One Vision*.

Relaxing in the studio in Munich, and for once not immersed in Scrabble,
there is no escaping the camera for Freddie. A documentary on the band
was being filmed at this time, hence the reluctant tolerance of camera-crew
presence during the making of a Queen recording. Usually the band
worked in strict privacy – just the four of them, and producer/engineer.

Top: Discussing the intricacies of guitar parts for *One Vision*, Brian and Freddie work their particular magic and soon 'nail it'! Extracts of this fascinating encounter can be seen on Queen's *Magic Years* video documentary (released in 1987).

Bottom: Still striving for perfection on *One Vision*, Freddie and Roger thrash out further ideas.

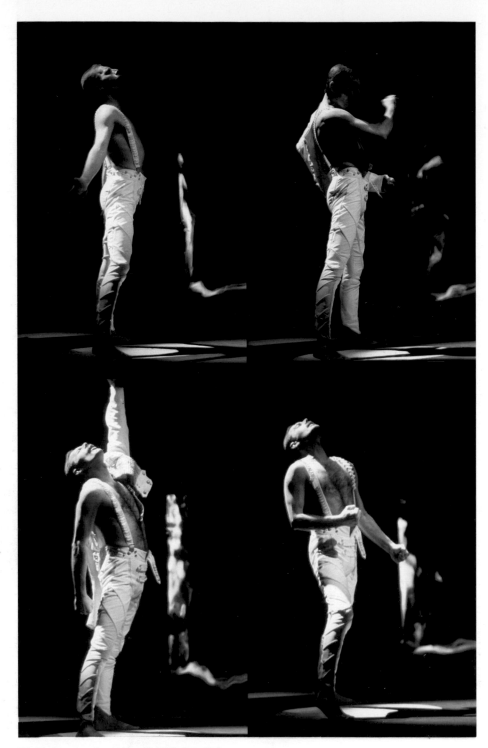

Filming the promotional video for *I Was Born To Love You* in 1985, Freddie, amid the shimmering mirrors he conceived, gets into the performance. Like so many great Queen/Freddie epics, this video was directed by David Mallet.

and it's a very different gift. It was fantastic singing on stage with her. What an experience! It really was a dream come true and just before we went on stage I couldn't help wondering if all this was really happening to me. And though I knew I was taking a big chance doing something like that, it gave me such a fantastic rush.

I was a wreck, but then so was she. I was bringing her into my rock'n'roll world and so she was shaking like a leaf, and saying, "Will they accept me?" She asked me how we should do it and I said, "Oh, we should just stand there and deliver the song," which is how operatic recitals are done. I had to sort of restrain myself too. I had to keep in mind that I couldn't do all my usual balletic stuff, none of those prancy poses, and all that. No, I had to just deliver it in a fucking tuxedo – which I'd never done in front of an audience before – and just go for it! It was strange for me to be wearing a tuxedo, but did you see her flying about all over the place?

The atmosphere was amazing. It was such a drag about my voice letting me down, because as we were set to perform I started having difficulties, so I didn't want to risk singing live. It's a very difficult thing for me because they're complex songs and we just didn't have enough rehearsal time as well. We did think we might do something live but my God, I tell you, it would need a LOT of rehearsal – weeks and weeks of it.

I'm used to singing with Queen, where hiding behind their power is quite easy to do. But here, each note counts and it's a very different kind of discipline. I can do it in a studio because I can have re-takes, but I wondered whether I could do it live, where you have to do it straight away. She's used to that, whereas I'm not. I've never done things with orchestras, and if my voice was not to come up to scratch I'd be letting her down. I wouldn't want to take any chances.

When it was all over I thought, "I've gone out of my way to try these things, and to see them come to fruition is just wonderful." I didn't think I was capable of writing operatic pieces that would suit a world renowned prima donna. I really didn't know I was capable of things such as that. I thought "What else is there left for me to do?" I mean, I defy any other rock'n'roll personality living today to duet with a legendary opera diva, and survive!

I think my solo work probably brought Queen closer together and enhanced our careers. I had no doubt that Queen would come back even bigger. I have a very good outlet within the group, so I'm not stifled in any way and I'm certainly not complaining. It would have been very easy for me at one stage to become a solo artist, because the draw was there. People in the media were always asking when I would go it alone. But I was very happy with Queen, and therefore I didn't need to give my ego a boost by suddenly leaving them and becoming solo. It's a very tempting area for me but why ruin the damn thing? I feel a loyalty towards the band and I'd hate to let them down. That, to me, is too high a price.

Chapter nine

CRAZY PERFORMANCE

*"Singing upside down with the Royal
Ballet was a wonderful thrill."*

I like ballet. It's theatre, and that's the kind of entertainment I like. The audience is so different and I like to see how a performer, an entertainer, puts it across in other situations. I know that rock'n'roll artists are very raucous, but that doesn't mean I can't go and listen to something like Montserrat Caballé doing a recital in New York, which I did, to pin-drop silence. She had no microphone or anything. You can learn a lot from that, how they train, the kind of lighting they use, the sets – it's all research, and it's all useful.

I've always tried to incorporate those styles into my work, but to say that I'm very well equipped in ballet dancing is totally wrong. I can't dance for shit, my dears! I cheat a lot and I'm very limited, so on stage I just use my limitations to the full. I did a sort of mock ballet and I knew that at that time to introduce a balletic feel into rock and roll was outrageous. What was a funky rock and roll audience going to say about this prancing ballerina coming on? But I thought, "I'll sing my songs with a tutu on, I don't care," because it's basically a form of outrage and shock.

I only really knew about ballet from watching it on television, but I always enjoyed what I saw. Then I became very good friends with Sir Joseph Lockwood, at EMI, who was also Chairman of the Royal Ballet board of governors. I began to meet people who were involved in ballet and I became more and more fascinated by them. I finally saw Baryshnikov dance with the American Ballet Theatre and he was just mind-blowing – more than Nureyev, more than anyone. I mean he could really fly, and when I saw him on stage I was so in awe that I felt like a groupie.

It all started for me when the Royal Ballet then asked me to dance with them, in 1979, and I thought they were mad! But in the end I did a charity gala with them. As far as I can recall, it's the only time that rock'n'roll has actually ventured into the ballet world... a dabble in an area where most rock'n'rollers would freak out.

After finding out what it involved, it really scared me, to be honest. I can't be choreographed; I'm hopeless at that, I really am. Their whole thing is choreographed; you've got to learn the steps and actually recreate them every night when you perform, or otherwise other things will go wrong. Whereas, on my stage, I have that freedom and I have learned to be able to do what I want, at whatever given point, depending on how I feel. So that's why when I was put in that kind of framework with the ballet people, and they asked me to go through a certain set of movements, I found it exceptionally difficult. I said, "I just can't do it." I suppose because they'd seen me on stage they automatically assumed I was a worthwhile dancer.

Still, they had me rehearsing all kinds of dance steps and there I was at the barre bending and stretching my legs. I was trying to do, in a few days, the kinds of things they had spent years perfecting, and let me tell you, it was murder. After two days I was in agony. I was aching in places I didn't even know I had. Then, when the night of the gala came, I was just amazed at the backstage scenes. When I had my entrances to do I had to fight my way through Merle Park and Anthony Dowell and all these people, and say, "Excuse me, I'm going on now." It was outrageous.

I did this very exotic leap, fell into the dancers' arms, and they carried me across the stage as I was still singing. I still don't believe I did that. It was spectacular and the house went quite wild. I wasn't quite Baryshnikov, but it wasn't bad for an ageing beginner.

We did *Bohemian Rhapsody* and *Crazy Little Thing Called Love*, and it was nice to put the same songs across in a totally different way and find it could be accepted. I put a bit of rock'n'roll into the ballet and it gave me a great thrill. But it was also the most nerve-racking thing for me, and I was shivering in the wings. It's always the case when you're put outside of your normal sphere, it's much harder, but I always like a challenge. I'd like to see Mick Jagger or Rod Stewart trying something like that.

I think the Royal Ballet people enjoyed it too, and it gave them the chance to loosen up as well. They didn't have to conform to the classical roles and they love doing all that. In fact, they said they'd love to come on tour with Queen and do it the other way round. They would do it like a shot, but I think there's a time and place for everything. At the time, we were doing very macho rock'n'roll, and all those things, and it just wouldn't go.

I did it just to keep me interested, to be honest, but I was very happy doing what I do with Queen. You couldn't suddenly say, at 32, "I want to be a ballet dancer!" At least, that's my excuse.

Chapter ten

TO THRILL YOU WE'LL USE ANY DEVICE

"We started the video boom remember!"

Bohemian Rhapsody was one of the first videos to get the kind of attention that videos get now, and it only cost about five thousand pounds. It's big business now, and it's a very good way of showcasing yourself.

We decided we should put *Rhapsody* on film and let people see it. We didn't know how it was going to be looked upon or how they were going to receive it. To us it was just another form of theatre. But it just went crazy, and since then everybody's been doing it. In the early days you would make an album, then you did a tour straight afterwards, but sometimes it was 4 or 5 months before you got to a country. We recognised that a video could get to a lot of people in a lot of countries without you actually being there, and you could release a record and a video simultaneously. It became very fast and it helped record sales greatly.

It now seems that videos are more important than radio. It's the downside of MTV. Every time you hear a song you automatically picture the video. You do get so much more insight into the song and you also get a feel of maybe how the artist wanted it. But, there is a danger that the buyer might be misguided. Once, when you heard a piece of music you used to have to conjure up an image for yourself, but the moment you make a video people are saying, "Oh my God, *that's* the way he wants to put it across." It really narrows it down.

Somebody once came up to me and told me he had a pre-conceived idea of what he thought I was telling him in a song, but when he saw the video it was totally wrong. He said that he'd totally lost all meaning of what I was trying to say. But there you go! I wasn't upset, but it's sad that they'll always be some people who are going to be disillusioned by the fact that the video is not cohesive with the song in terms of what they wanted to see.

Nowadays you have to look good in films, as well. You've got to have a good image. I think one of the nicest bands around are The Police. To me, they've captured it. They've got that image and I think that's what really started them going. I love them. They're very good.

Look at us, look at David Bowie… You *have* to have an image, but that doesn't sell records all the time. A strong image is very important for longevity. Today it's Boy George and Annie Lennox, and when we started there was Roxy Music and David Bowie, and various others. It was a very strong image for that time. Think what The Beatles started in their time. I mean, to have that kind of hair and that look, then, was the same kind of impact. It was just a different time and a different perspective.

Promotional videos might help song writing, actually. I think it's going to be very commonplace where people start recording, even writing, with the video in mind – which is wonderful. It's another dimension.

A lot of the time people make videos and expect musicians to act a certain role, and that's where it falls down. There have been a lot of times where we've shied away from that. If you go into a little acting thing you've got to do it really well, and if you don't it just comes across as really crass. You've got to be very careful.

I think *I Want To Break Free* [1984] works because of the fun element and the comedy. It's so farcical. I can't think of another video where the four principals, as it were, are actually doing real comedy drag. So often Queen comes across as very serious, when there is actually a lot of tongue-in-cheek there that people miss. The music ability is always there, and we've always been humorous underneath, but maybe it doesn't come across through songs

103

– and on stage when we're very aggressive. The humour element is always lost. That video was a good way of showcasing that side of us, and I think we coped quite well.

I was dying to dress up in drag. Doesn't everybody? It was just one of those things. I'm sure everybody thought it was my idea, but in fact it wasn't my idea at all. It came from Roger, and actually the other three *ran* into their frocks quicker than anything. It's obvious that that's something I would do, but because it was their idea it came across a lot better. If it had been me, it would have been that much harder for them to accept the role, and I don't think it would have worked.

It wasn't a literal take-off of Coronation Street, it just came from that era. But if somebody had put us together and put names underneath us, well then I realised I had become Bet Lynch. Actually I thought I was more Finella Fielding, to be honest. Really, that wig was superb. It was Finella, although I do like Bet Lynch. She's one of my favourites – and Hilda Ogden of course.

I think that's one of our best videos to date. In fact it still makes me chuckle every time I see it, and I've seen it a lot of times. I'm glad we did it. People were quite amazed by the fact we could fool around and drag up and still be good musicians. In America it wasn't accepted at all well because they still regarded us as the heavy rockers there – the macho thing. They reacted with, "What are my idols doing dressing up in frocks?" There's a big risk element involved with most things we do, and I think our staunchest fans will know that we can come up with all sorts of ridiculous things. Some of them will work, and some don't, but I think the rest of the group will take my view on this… that we don't give a damn. We do what we want to do, and it's either accepted or not.

When it comes to videos I like to have fun in them. If you do that it comes across and people can relate to that. Basically it's just me having fun. I can't just sit in a chair knitting a blouse, or whatever, I have to go through all these horrible scenes and things which is what I'm all about. So in a funny way they are parts of my life that I'm just putting into pictures.

I Was Born To Love You [1985] is basically a romp through my house. That's what I do every night, so that came very easily. The dancing is quite heavy and some of the out-takes are even heavier than the parts you see. The idea in that story was that I had to slap the girl hard, and all that, but I was just going through the motions and she found she couldn't perform. I had to actually hit her, and kick her properly, and throw her around, so that she could come back at me and make it believable. When we saw it back I realised I couldn't have that it in my video, as nobody would show it, so we just used little snatches of it, but even so MTV found it hard to relate.

A lot of that video is on a set with me in front of all these mirrored images that were going to be static. Then I suddenly thought, "Why don't we have people stand behind them and just shake them a little, and see what kind of effect we get?" It was a very cheap way of getting the effect but sometimes these things just happen to be the best thing at the right time. So that wasn't actually thought out on paper. We had wanted static images of me, but then suddenly all this shimmering happened at the back, and it worked.

With *I'm Going Slightly Mad* [1991], I wanted to make that video as memorable as possible. I've always wanted to co-star in a video with a gorilla and a group of penguins. A little bit of Queen madness was required!

Most of the stuff I do is pretending. It's like acting... I go on stage and pretend to be a macho man and all those things. I think *The Great Pretender* is a great title for what I do because I *am* The Great Pretender! I've always had that in the back of my mind and that song is the one I've always wanted to cover. I went into the studio [in 1987] and tried a few trials, and I liked it. It suited my voice and it's a great song to sing. And, in my videos I go through all the different characters and I'm pretending again.

I've always believed that in the end, in terms of videos, that no matter how good your image is, the song has to be good too. The song has got to be good because people buy the song. They don't buy the image all the time, because you're actually only doing all that to sell the song. You can only hype the public up to a certain point.

I think Boy George has got a great image, but it doesn't matter how good your image is or how wonderful the video is, if his songs weren't any good they wouldn't sell. Even if he wore a teapot on his head, which he keeps saying he will, it wouldn't matter.

Chapter eleven

TU VOZ PENETRA EN MI

"I'm not a star-fucker.
How can I be a star-fucker?
I am a star!"

I listen to all kinds of music, from Jimi Hendrix and George Michael, to Liza Minnelli and Aretha Franklin, all the way back to Mae West.

Jimi Hendrix was just a beautiful man, a master showman and a dedicated musician. I would scour the country to see him whenever he played because he really had everything any rock and roll star should have; all the style and presence. He didn't have to force anything. He'd just make an entrance and the whole place would be on fire. He was living out everything I wanted to be.

I think on stage you either have the magic, or you don't, and there's no way you can work up to it. Liza Minnelli just oozes with sheer talent. She has energy and stamina, which she gets across on stage, and the way she delivers herself to the public is a good influence. There is a lot to learn from her.

I would say that Led Zeppelin are the greatest, and Robert Plant is one of the most original vocalists of our time. As a rock band they deserved the kind of success they got.

I love the Queen of Soul, Aretha Franklin, above all other singers. She must have one of the best voices *ever* and she sings like a dream. I wish I could sing half as well as she does. It's so natural and she puts her whole emotion into it. Each word she sings is so full of meaning and expression. I could listen to it forever.

I'd love Aretha to sing *Somebody To Love*, actually. That would be a nice thing. But as for me trying to sing with her? Well, she hasn't approached me yet!

I'm mad that George Michael did a duet with her. I could have done it better! Mind you, having said that, I think George Michael has a very good voice, too. He's one of the singers that I like.

I also liked Tears For Fears, because they wrote music I could really relate to. They had a lot of rhythm and at the same time a lot of aggression. Flo & Eddie were simply a riot, I liked them. I enjoy Joni Mitchell tremendously, and am constantly awed by her vocal phrasing as well as the amazing things she writes. Frankie Goes To Hollywood were a tremendous act, and so were Spandau Ballet, while Barbara Valentine fascinated me because she's got such great tits!

I think the Human League are one of the best bands around, and The Police – I think they're very good. They're an excellent band and they've got the ingredients that you need. I didn't like the Thompson Twins though. I don't know the real reason why, it's just one of those things.

It would be nice to see a bigger influx of British acts, actually, taking over America like they used to. I think nowadays bands come up at a rapid pace and then fizzle out at a rapid pace, which is a bit sad. Some of the newer bands seem to want to get up there very quickly, and think they've made it over night. What they don't realise is that after they've conquered England, to be an international success, you've really got to slog in America too. You may be number one in England, and you're the bees knees there, but probably America hasn't even heard of you.

I think the standards in music are so high these days and the competition is so great. But I like that, because otherwise people like me get too complacent. Every couple of years there's a sifting process and the really good bands stay, and all the crap gets left behind. That happens all the time. But if you ask me what shape it's all going to be in in the future, nobody can tell you that.

Boy George has great talent. I like him very much. We became good friends. That boy's so brave – he did such a lot to make society more tolerant about sexual preferences. When I started, rock bands all wore dirty jeans, and then suddenly there I was in a Zandra Rhodes frock and make up. It was totally outrageous. Boy George just updated the whole glam rock bit, but he did it in his own individual way.

He has got staying power, which is a heavy ingredient that you need to have. I think he is going to be here for a long while. You can always tell when someone is going to stay, and Boy George is going to stay. A lot of people blow out because of the pressure one gets from being in the public eye like that, but the one thing I do know about George is that he does love publicity. He just wants publicity at all costs and even seems to thrive on adverse publicity. Well that's his thing, and I just hope he comes through it ok.

I have friends in the music business and I like being in that company now and again, but I don't go out of my way to go to every reception just to be seen. No no no. My God, no! There was a time when I used to do that kind of thing because it was part of learning the career, and you have to go through all that. It's something that you'd be a liar to say you didn't do.

When you start off you want to be a star, so you want to be associated with bigger stars. It's a growth process that has to happen. But I found out it can be empty, it can be cruel, and it can be rotten. You learn by your mistakes, but it's up to you to opt out or you just carry on being like that until you burn yourself out. It's something that didn't agree with me, and I just learned that there are other things in life besides just being seen out with a superstar on each arm.

I've never been very good at it anyway. When I was introduced to Prince Andrew I was wearing a white scarf and holding a glass of wine. I was so

109

nervous I didn't realise my scarf was dangling in the drink. There I was trying to be really cool and suddenly the Prince said, "Freddie, I don't think you really want this getting wet." And he squeezed out the scarf and that broke the ice between us. I said, "Thank goodness you've put me at ease... Now I can use the odd bit of dirty language." Then we both burst out laughing. He really got into the spirit of things and even had a dance. He's really quite hip in those situations and I have a lot of respect for royalty. I'm a tremendous patriot.

I'm very close with a lot of people – like David Bowie and Elton John. Elton's a good old cookie, isn't he? I love him to death and I think he's fabulous. To me he's like one of those last Hollywood actresses of any worth. He has been a pioneer in rock'n'roll. The first time I met him he was wonderful, one of those people you can instantly get on with. He said he liked *Killer Queen* and anyone who says that goes in my white book. My black book is bursting at the seams!

Rod Stewart, Elton John and I were going to form a band, once upon a time, called Hair, Nose and Teeth – after the three of us. We'd meet up from time to time at parties or dinners, and we just thought that we should sing together. But I think that getting three people like us in a studio would be like throwing in a bomb and waiting for it to explode. It's nice when you've had a lot of wine and you talk about it and say, "Yes, let's do it," but the next day, when you're sober and Elton says, 'I'm not gonna sing with Rod," and Rod says, "I'm not gonna sing with Freddie," and I say, "Well, I'm not gonna sing with Elton!' you realise it's never going to happen. Besides, none of our egos could agree on the order of the words! Naturally I would want it to be called Teeth, Nose and Hair, and the others would want it the other way around. So there you go! But if it ever comes about, I will buy the album.

I'm very fond of Rod and Elton. They both came to my last birthday party and sang happy birthday when the cake was wheeled in. I shouted out, "This is probably the first time the two of you have sung without being paid for it!"

When we were in Los Angeles working on the Queen album *The Works*, Rod was in town and he came in and we just started jamming. He sang on a song I'd written*. It was all done on the spur of the moment in the same way that David Bowie and Queen did *Under Pressure*. He just came in the studio and we were fooling around, and it snowballed, and eventually turned into a song. So these are things that you can't plan, because if you tried they would never happen.

I think all the other Queen members would agree that because we have been working together for so long, we know each other instinctively now. I even write songs in terms of Queen. I know exactly what the bass player is capable of, and the guitarist and drummer, and things like that. But to work with another established artist, like when we did our thing with David Bowie, you're working from stage one, and that's a great challenge. You don't know which way to write, you don't know what kind of aggression you're going to get, what kind of compliment you're going to get, or what kind of rapport you're going to achieve. So when you're working with other people the best way is just to go in there and do it. If it sparks off, you've got it, otherwise you just forget it.

I'm always quite interested in working with other musicians, people like Michael Jackson. Although she's a worry. All that money and no taste, my dears! What a waste! We had three tracks in the can, but unfortunately they were never finished. They were great songs but the problem was time – as we were both very busy at that period. We never seemed to be in the same country long enough to actually finish everything completely. One of the songs was called *State of Shock*, and Michael even called me to ask if I could complete it, but I couldn't because I had commitments with Queen. Mick Jagger took over instead. It was a shame, but ultimately a song is a song. As long as the friendship is there, that's what matters.

I'd like to release something with Michael because he is a really marvellous person to work with. He has been a friend of ours for a long while. He used to come and see our shows all the time, and that is how the friendship grew. We were always interested in each other's styles. I would regularly play him the new Queen album when it was cut and he would play me his stuff. We kept saying, "Why don't we do something together?"

---

*This later became *Let Me Live* on Queen's final album *Made In Heaven*, 1995, without any of Rod Stewart's vocals.

Just think, I could have been on *Thriller*. Think of the royalties I've missed out on!

Michael and I grew apart a bit after his massive success with *Thriller* [1983]. He simply retreated into a world of his own. We used to have great fun going to clubs together but now he won't come out of his fortress and it's very sad. He's so worried someone will do him in that he's paranoid about absolutely everything. I get worried myself, but I'll never let it take over my life like that.

He's the biggest thing ever in terms of sales, and that brings a very different kind of pressure because he has been singled out as the best. That is hard for even me to relate to. I think he's an enigma, and that makes him a God-given gift to the media because they can write anything about him because it all fits. He's very shy and all I can say is that at the time when I knew him he was a very nice and sweet guy, and very talented. That's it.

I have my friends and I don't care where they come from or what they do for a living. I don't go out of my way to say my friends should only be musicians because I enjoy all sorts of characters. We don't have to talk about music, I just like interesting people who actually have more to talk about than just music. I can talk about all kinds of things – like dirt and filth.

I think I get on with most people. I'm sure I'd even get on with King Kong very well. We're the same age. Mind you, I've climbed higher buildings than that!

Chapter twelve

ONE MAN, ONE GOAL, ONE VISION

*"I suppose that's what Bob Geldof is at the moment,
the Mother Theresa of rock'n'roll."*

I think Live Aid is a very good cause. We have done things for charity before – we've all done individual charity things in the past, I'm sure – but this is an immense effort, a community effort, where all of us are doing it together.

I think Bob Geldof has done a wonderful thing in actually sparking it off. I'm sure we all had it in us to do that, but it took someone like him to actually drive it. It is like a driving force, to get us all to come together. To get some of the biggest stars in the world together at one event is quite a feat

When I first saw the television report it disturbed me so deeply I couldn't bear to watch it. I had to switch the television off. I don't like to dwell on it. I know it's there. There's that thing where you just sit back and think, "Well, what can I do?" Unless you think you're the Mother Theresa of rock'n'roll and can suddenly rush out there and organise something. I suppose that's what Bob Geldof is at the moment, the Mother Theresa of rock'n'roll.

I have never felt guilty about being rich, and those feelings weren't there when I decided to perform in Live Aid. What I felt was sheer sorrow and a deep upset that something like this was going on in our world, and I felt for a time quite, quite helpless. The point of this concert is to wake people up to the starvation and famine, to make everyone realise just what is going on, and to do something positive that will hopefully touch people and make them dig into their pockets.

You don't have to identify with poverty on that level to give money or to help people. Why should you? Sometimes it is very black and white. Some people have money and they want to help the ones in need.

I don't think that people should actually think in terms of the British helping Africa, as it were, or, "Why don't we look on our own doorstep first?" I think something as large as this should be universal. We shouldn't have any kind of parallels. We shouldn't be looking at it in terms of us and them. It should be all of us. I think when people are starving, we are all humans and we should be looked upon as one.

I'm quite a generous person. If I can do anything in my little ways, I do it. In terms of money, I have enough. I'm not afraid of giving it to other people, as long as it gets to the right places.

It's a little bit like when I did the ballet thing for Save the Children. And I remember also there was a charity event where Queen songs were performed at the Albert Hall, to benefit leukaemia research, and it was attended by one of the royals. I remember we did the first one, then I think the Beatles did the second one, and McCartney attended it, and the Queen. And Joan Collins sang *Imagine* – which was dreadful, apparently!

I would have loved to have been on the original Band Aid record, to have participated in that too, but I only heard about it when we were in Germany. And I don't know if they would have had me on the record anyway. I'm a bit old. And then when the American one came out, the way all those stars gelled together, well that was superb. I think it sort of snowballed into this Live Aid concert, which is very nice. And then Bob actually called Brian up and it went from there. I think we thought that we shouldn't be left out.

Queen seems to be in various parts of the globe quite a bit, so this time, being in the country at the right time, we made an effort to say, "Ok, we'd better make sure that on this date [July 13th 1985] we're free." We're looking forward to doing it.

Live Aid is going to be chaotic. It has to be. I mean we're not all wonderfully behaved kids, are we? That's actually going to be the nice part of it. Lots of friction, and we're all going to try and out-do each other.

We're just going to go on there and play. We're going to be doing our best songs. At the moment we haven't decided exactly which ones, but I think we're going to do bits of *Rhapsody* and *Champions*. Basically you're not trying to put across your *new* material or anything. No, you hit them with your best-known material.

Brian and I were thinking about poverty going on all around the world and that's why *Is This The World We Created* came about. I think for Live Aid we're actually going to do that as a special thing, right at the end. And the funny thing is it was written before, but it seems to fit in quite well.

It's very odd, but we composed that particular song well before the Live Aid project. It was a song we wrote about the suffering and starvation of children all over the planet, and it matched the situation so well that we decided it was definitely one song we would do.

I tell you, when it comes to that duet, *Is This The World We Created*, it's an integral part of what's going on, and the song seems to convey a lot of what the event is about. I think that's probably going to bring tears to my eyes when we do it. I'll have to make sure I do it properly.

It's amazing, the first line is 'Just look at all those hungry mouths we have to feed.' I can't believe it. It's as if someone actually asked us to write a song for this event, but we had one already. Actually it was Jim Beach's idea. Jim thought of it. Because it was there, all written, and that's why they've given us a special spot.

We want to perform all the songs that people are familiar with and can identify with. The concert may have come out of a terrible human tragedy, but we want to make it a joyous occasion. It's not a promotional thing.

To be honest, let's face it, all us rock stars still want to be in the limelight and this is going to showcase us. Let's be open about it. Ok we're helping out, but from the other point of view it's going to be a worldwide audience, an all over simultaneous broadcast. That's what we're all about as well and we shouldn't forget that. I doubt there is one artist that's going to appear who hasn't realised that fact. So there's that to consider as well.

I don't think I'd be doing it out of guilt. Even if I didn't do it the poverty would still be there. It's something that will always be there. We'll do all we can do to help because it's a wonderful thing. But as far as I'm concerned I'm doing it out of pride. It's something to be proud of – that I'm actually in with all the biggies – all the biggest stars – and that I can do something worthwhile. Yes, I'm proud more than anything.

Sometimes you do feel helpless, and I think this is my way of showing that I can do my bit. And that's as far as I want to go.

Chapter thirteen

THIS IS THE ONLY LIFE FOR ME

"People are apprehensive when they meet me and they think
I'm going to eat them. But underneath it all I'm quite shy
and very few people know what I'm really like."

I remember there was a time and place in the early days where of course I wanted to be looked upon, so therefore you dress accordingly. I wore Zandra Rhodes dresses and painted my fingernails black, and I wore eye make up and had long hair. I wore women's blouses and then I would walk into a room and close it dead. That's the way to make an entrance, and you can do that. Those things you can do if you're in that position. And now, having gone through a lot, I want my privacy.

I hate mixing with lots of showbiz personalities. I could do a Rod Stewart and join that crowd but I want to stay out of all that. I'm not one of those people who like to go to press receptions because I like to keep myself to myself more than anything. In the early days I used to enjoy being recognised, but not now. When I'm not in Queen I want to be the ordinary man in the street.

There are times when I wake up in the morning and I think, "My God, I wish I wasn't Freddie Mercury today!" I'm in the public eye whether I like it or not, but I don't want everything I do to be made public. I'm a virgo, I'm like Greta Garbo, I want to be left alone. I am a bit reclusive but it's not a calculated thing. I like to be alone and shut myself off with my friends, but I'd hate to be on a desert island. I would loathe that. I do like people around me but I like them in *my* environment. I've got all my friends that come to me and maybe it's a very selfish thing to do, but it's a wonderful treat for me.

People are the main thing, but I have to be surrounded by something, even if it's just object d'art. So, I collect a lot, and my whole house is filled with beautiful Japanese art and antiques. That's also why I want lots of fish, and lots of cats. I suppose it's a sort of shy outlook.

I can take numerous risks in the music world because that's a world I live in where I have no boundaries. But I won't take risks in terms of my social life. I have to be totally comfortable in a social situation before I step into it and that can make me seem a very boring person. I think I probably socialise more when I'm in different parts of the world because I like to see different things and I find London a bit lacking. I suppose it's because it's home, and when I'm there I like to stay at home. But when I'm touring, I have some of the best times because I get to see new places and I'm not afraid of going to new events. I'm quite nosey. People tell me about things and I like to find out for myself.

I was a very insecure young boy, probably because I was a bit sheltered. My uncle had a villa in Dar-Es-Salem only yards from the sea, and in the morning I'd be woken by the servant. Clutching an orange juice, I'd literally step out on to the beach. In a way I've been very fortunate, even in the early days. I love being pampered, it's just something that's grown with me.

I was also a precocious child and my parents thought boarding school would do me good. So, when I was about seven, I was put in one in India for a while. It was an upheaval of an upbringing, which seems to have worked, I guess.

Of course there were feelings of being sent away from my parents and sister whom I missed very much – feelings of loneliness, feelings of being rejected – but you had to do what you were told, so the sensible thing was to make the most of it. I was put in an environment where I had to fend for myself, so I got a good grasp of how to be responsible at an early age, and I think that's what's made me into such a fiend.

One thing boarding schools teaches you, is how to fend for yourself, and I did that from the start. It taught me to be independent and not to rely on anybody else. All the things they say about boarding schools are more or less true, about all the bullying and everything else.

I loathed cricket and long-distance running; I was completely useless at both! But I could sprint, I was good at hockey, and I was just brilliant in the boxing ring... believe it or not.

I had the odd schoolmaster chasing me, but it didn't shock me because somehow at boarding school you're not confronted by it, you are just slowly aware of it. There were times when I was young and green. I had a crush on a master, and would have done anything for him. It's a thing schoolboys go through, and I had my share of schoolboy pranks, but I'm not going to elaborate any further.

I took piano lessons at school and really enjoyed it. That was my mother's doing. She made sure I stuck at it and I did it up to grade four classical, practical and theory. At first I kept up the lessons because I knew she wanted me to, but then I really grew to love playing. I basically play by ear and I can't sight read at all. I don't need it. I leave that to the others. It's not like Mozart, is it? We reach more people this way.

I think I always liked to sing but I didn't look upon it as a career. When I was a little baby I was in the choir and I just liked to sing. I would copy Elvis Presley songs, then I suddenly realised that I could actually write songs and make my own music. Call it a natural gift, or whatever.

Later I went to Ealing Art School, the year after Pete Townshend left. Music was a sideline to everything we did and the school was a breeding ground for musicians. I got my diploma and then I thought I'd chance it as a freelance artist. I did it for a couple of months but then I thought, "My God, I've done enough." The interest just wasn't there. And the music thing just grew and grew. Finally I said, "Right, I'm taking the plunge – it's music." I'm one of those people who believes in doing things that interest you. Music is so interesting, my dears.

Am I vain? To a certain extent, yes. I have those ingredients. I like to feel that I look good at all times when I go out. I think it's inner happiness. It has to come from within. For me, happiness is the most important thing, and if I'm happy then it shows in my work. My happiness is defined in many ways. Just buying somebody a gift is wonderful, but at the same time performing to an audience fulfils me. I wouldn't be in this business if I didn't like it.

I think most people like me go through phases, and sometimes I have very bad patches. But I don't have as many problems as I did before, when I was just bogged down by things. I used to attack each problem as it came. It was a big thing with me and I had to cross that hurdle otherwise I couldn't survive, I couldn't do anything else. Now I think I've grown up and learnt how to deal with them. I don't let it worry me because I take my good times when I get them and I live from day to day, I really do.

Certainly I'm a flamboyant person, and I like to live life. I certainly work hard for it, and I want to have a good time. It might not come again, so I want to enjoy myself a little. Now I'm not scared to do what I want to do and I'm not worried if I make a fool of myself. If I fall into a dustbin, which I have done many times, I don't worry about the fact, if I'm having a good time.

Boredom and dullness are the biggest diseases in the whole world, dears. You can never say that life with me is boring. Excess is a part of my nature and I really need danger and excitement. I was often warned to stay away from clubs because they are too dangerous. But I revel in that. I'm never scared of putting myself out on a limb. I was not made for just sitting and watching television. I love to surround myself with strange and interesting people because they make me feel more alive. Extremely straight people bore me stiff. I love freaky people. By nature I'm restless and highly-strung, so I wouldn't make a good family man.

I don't do things by halves. I can shift from one extreme to the other quite easily. I don't like anything in between. Grey has never been a favourite colour of mine. I sort of change from day to day like a chameleon. Each day is different to me and I look forward to that because I don't want to be the same person every day.

I can't relax in bed all day and just do nothing. I hardly read books because I think that's a waste of time. I relax in ways most people can't understand, by just sleeping on a plane when I'm flying for 20 minutes. That's all the relaxation I need. I don't need tons of sleep, I can get by with 3 or 4 hours sleep a night. That's enough for me. I recharge my batteries in that short a time and I'm up again.

I have to be doing something every day. I want to earn my keep. I can't sit still for long, and if you know that you need constant entertainment, you make sure you have it. I may just be being greedy, but I'm an entertainer... It's in the blood. I'm a trouper, so give me a stage. But in a way I've created a monster and I'm the one who has to live with it. I'm probably going to go mad in a few years time. I'm going to be one of those insane musicians.

I'm driven by my work and will go on for as long as my system will allow me. The things that I admire the most are the things that require total dedication, twelve hours of work a day, and sleepless nights. I'm not the only one. I think Phil Collins is a prime example because he's a real workaholic too.

People think I'm a real... it starts with 'C', but I can't say that... and it's not a cherub! I'm very hard to deal with and, to some people, I'm a bitch. I actually enjoy being a bitch. I enjoy being surrounded by bitches. I certainly don't go looking for the most perfect people because I'd find that boring. I'm like a mad dog about town and I like to enjoy life. But now I actually pay more attention to making people realise that I am normal. It's such a shit thing when people think, "Oh Freddie Mercury, he won't talk to me!" But you see it's a fine dividing line because when people believe that you've got all this money and success, but you're still going to be one of the lads, then they tread all over you. Then you have to stop and say, "I'm still a fucking star, you respect me, but I can still have a cup of tea and a boogie with you." It's just a matter of discipline.

You always have a certain idea of what you are all about, and I think that my character on stage is totally different to my character off stage. There are various aspects of me. Generally I'm likeable, I think, but I can change and be very moody and obnoxious. I think every character is made up of a load of ingredients, and I'm no different. There are no half measures with me, and that can be precarious because somebody can tread all over me, which has happened a lot of times. But then sometimes I'm a big, macho, sexual object, and I'm very arrogant. Then, *nobody* can get through to me.

I'm not perfect by any means, but I live in a fair way. I'm sometimes too lenient, that's my problem. I'm a very possessive person, but I want to have my cake and eat it too. Once I find someone's betrayed me, I go the other way, and become an ogre. I'm very hard on the exterior but very soft-centred, like a chocolate – something out of Black Magic.

These images that I've portrayed over the years are a kind of pretence. I wore costumes and put myself in different atmospheres and characters, but underneath that there is a real me. I've been pretending all this time, wearing bananas on my head, wearing glitter and coming on stage on someone's shoulders. I like to ridicule myself and I don't take myself too seriously. I wouldn't wear these clothes if I was serious. The one thing that keeps me going is that I like to laugh at myself. But it is all a pretence. Underneath it, I'm still a musician.

I have all kinds of paranoia. Being alone is one. I can't go anywhere on my own. I always have to have someone with me whenever I'm shopping, probably because I don't like being stared at. I don't care who stares at me, but I don't like people who are a bit rude, who just come up to me, because nobody likes that.

Everyone has their moments, putting on airs and graces. I mean, I never tie my own shoe laces. Never. It's just not the done thing in rock'n'roll. My dears, I'm the vainest creature going. I do work out sometimes, although I don't like going to the actual gym. It's a bit embarrassing, especially when there's all these big blokes looking at a weed trying to pick up the odd dumb-bell. Also I don't like the way my teeth protrude. I'm going to have them done, but I just haven't had the time. Apart from that... I'm perfect. Seriously though, I'm quite genuine inside. I don't set myself above others, I hate that kind of shit, I really do. I think my closest friends around me know that they can actually tease me and put me down.

It's a growth process. People grow up, and after all these years you have to be seen to be growing up, so that the people who've grown up with you can't suddenly say, "My God, he's *still* got long hair, and he's *still* wearing black fingernails and a lady's blouse!" I mean, it's ridiculous, and I would feel ridiculous. Until recently, dressing casually meant changing from a black satin suit to a blue one. I do like to dress with some style.

I've always wanted to be my own boss and I always felt that I knew best. It sounds very precocious, but I knew what I wanted. And if it all ended tomorrow, I would do it all again on my own terms. I know it's all going come to an end one day, but I won't lose sleep over it every night. That's not the reason I'm in it. I'm in it for the challenge. I don't want it made too easy for me and nobody hands it to me on a silver platter. I'd hate that. And I'd refuse it anyway.

I never try to self-analyse myself, I hate that kind of thing and I don't even like having my palm read. I've had people call me and say, "Oh you must go and see *this* person, it's just so accurate." But that scares me, to be honest. I like to find out for myself. It would be so boring if I found out what was going to happen to me because then I'd spend my entire life trying to avoid it.

I'm one of those people that doesn't look back and dwell over spilt milk. If it's a mistake then I just think, "It's passed, it's over with." In the same way, you can't revel in success because you're only as good as your last record in this business. It works both ways, so if I came up with a real rotten apple, I wouldn't give a damn.

Everybody wants a kind of accolade whether it be in the music field or whatever, and that's the way I am. But I would be quite happy to be famous in a completely different way. It's success, that matters, and feeling the weight of success behind you, in any given form, whether it be as an oil tycoon or any sort of executive. I would always strive for that, so I'm not hung up on the fact that it has to be as a musician. It's a wonderful gift to have. Although...

I don't think I would be a car mechanic, and I'm useless at adding up sums and things like that. As far as science is concerned, I'm rubbish, and I'm not a handyman... oh no. I'm a useless bugger!

I know how to get the best out of me, and I would always find what talent I had and push that forward to try and gain some kind of recognition and success out of it. I'm in much more command of myself these days because I know what I want and what I don't want. I live for tomorrow. Fuck today, it's tomorrow. I'm not going to listen to people telling me how I should react. Nobody tells me what to do.

I don't think of myself as a legend. Me and legends don't get on. I'm just a little sweetheart... I'm a sweetie. To me a legend is somebody like Montserrat Caballé. She's the legend and I'm just an old tart. I don't want to draw parallels to anybody else, because I don't think I have a parallel.

Chapter fourteen

MY MELANCHOLY BLUES

I am so depressed by these people who *still* won't admit that everything we do simply drips with originality!

Chapter fifteen

A MAN MADE PARADISE

"I'm a city person. I'm not into all
this country air and cow dung!"

Every person who makes a lot of money has a dream they want to carry out, and I achieved that dream with this wonderful house.

Whenever I watched Hollywood movies set in plush homes with lavish décor, I wanted that for myself, and now I've got it. But to me it was much more important to get the damn thing than to actually go and live in it. I'm very much like that – once I get something I'm not that keen on it any more. I still love the house, but the real enjoyment is that I've achieved it.

It's an eight bedroom house in Kensington, West London. It's full of marble floors and mahogany staircases. It even has a garden that is three quarters of an acre... in Kensington! Can you believe it? Recently an Arab offered me four million pounds for it. I told Elton John and he said, "Quick, sell it to him and live in a pre-fab!" But it's my dream home and I don't care how much it costs me.

I'd been looking for a house for a long time. I'm not into yards and yards of acreage, I just wanted a beautiful house in reasonable sized grounds. I'm a city person. I'm not into all this country air and cow dung!

I just felt that I wanted to live in England again, having lived in New York and Munich. I wanted a country mansion in London, but it took me a long while. I'd been living in the same little Kensington flat for ages, so I phoned Mary from America and asked her to find a place. I saw the house, fell in love with it, and within half an hour it was mine. It was in a terrible state and with all the changes I made I wasn't able to move in for a year.

I call it my country house, in town. It's very secluded, with huge grounds, right in the middle of London. Once a month I would get inspired and go there with the architect. "Why don't we have this wall removed?" I asked once... Everybody groaned and the architect nearly died. I went in there sloshed one day, after a good lunch – there is a wonderful bedroom area at the top, I had three knocked into one palatial suite – and in a sort of haze, I said, inspired, "What would be nice, is a glass dome over the top of all this bedroom area." The architect flinched, but went rushing back to his pen and drawing pad.

Before all that, I decided at some point that I would like to live in New York. I love New York. It's wonderful. But when I came to thinking about living there, I thought, "Oh dear, it's terribly different!" You can't live in New York at the pace you do when you're travelling through it. I didn't like that idea. I'd have been dead within a week.

I was going to leave England and try it on a trial basis, so I actually went and looked at some apartments in West Avenue. I found a wonderful place that I almost bought. This is before Mrs Thatcher's Government came in. But then when we came back to England, she was in, and I just thought, "Well, why not!" But it was nothing to do with money.

Work had got to be too much. I got tired of the whole business and decided I really needed a long break. I had just bought an apartment in New York and I wanted to spend some time there. I spent a lot of time finding it and as soon as I bought it I moved in. So that took preference over my London house and I lived there for a while. I worked with Michael Jackson while living there.

I love New York. It's aggressive and challenging and of course interesting. I like Munich too, having spent a lot of time there. It's very safe there, and very beautiful. We recorded albums there and you realise how safe it is. Munich is like a village. I was there so long that after a while the people didn't even consider that I was around. They didn't really pester me at all. I have a lot of friends over there and they know who I am, but they just treat me as another human being and they've accepted me that way. And that to me is a very good way of relaxing. I don't want to have to shut myself up and hide. That's not what I want. I'd go spare. I'd go mad...even quicker.

I like to feel that I can do exactly the same kind of things as other people do, like socialising and having parties, but not have those burdens. If I completely remove myself from that, and still be in the same town, that's my way of relaxing. You can just walk anywhere and you don't have to worry about your car being parked anywhere. Over here, in London, there's always somebody who'll scratch your expensive car, and this and that, and you have to have your chauffeur stay with it. But that doesn't happen in Munich. I can actually walk the streets there. I can't even cross the road in England. I have to be in a car all the time. But New York is very unsafe, as you know, and I wouldn't dare walk around there. That's just being stupid. You have to be very cautious.

I love the clubs in New York. I remember once I wanted to go to a club called the Gilded Grape, which I'd heard was really exciting, but everyone told me I shouldn't go – or if I did, at least to make sure I had a fast bullet-proof car waiting for me outside. Everyone tried to warn me about this club, which of course made me all the more determined to go. Not long after we got there, a massive fight broke out which ended up at our table. Chairs were being smashed, fists were flying, there was blood everywhere. Billie [Jean King] was petrified, but I loved it. I told her not to worry, and as the fight raged I grabbed her and took her on to the dance-floor. It was much more fun than having some cosy dinner back at my hotel.

When I go to New York I just slut myself around. It is Sin city with a capital 'S'. But you have to come away at the right time, because the moment you stay a day later, it grips you. It's very hypnotic. It's all tripping in at eight or nine every morning, taking throat injections so I can still sing. It's a *real* place. I love it.'

Though he would shave it off later for other scenes in this video, *I Want To Break Free* from 1984, Freddie left his moustache in place for this main sequence – tongue-in-cheek as ever. Contrary to popular belief, dressing in drag for this wonderful shoot was NOT Freddie's idea… he just embraced it with every fibre!

Filming the *Radio Ga Ga* promo video (November 1983). Borrowing from and based heavily on Fritz Lang's *Metropolis* film, of 1926, the rally crowd hand clapping sequence became a trademark sight at Queen live performances, never more dramatically on show than at Live Aid. The clap-clap-punch 'thing' turned into a phenomenon all around the world - as much a part of the Queen show as *Bo Rhap*, dazzling lights and ENORMOUS sound! It even re-surfaced on the 2005 Queen + Paul Rodgers concerts.

Freddie on stage with Queen – be it in front of 2,000 or 200,000 people -
was an inexhaustible unstoppable whirling dervish. There was no holding
him back, no restraining him, nothing to do but stare in awe. Again, this
image captures a moment from the magical 1986 tour.

"Thank you, God bless and sweet dreams... you lot of tarts!" This was Freddie's actual parting comment at Queen's 1977 Earls Court gig in London – though he offered similar felicitations during much later concerts too. Only Freddie could get away with that – and he knew it! Here, another concert on the Magic tour ends too soon and Freddie thanks the adoring masses once more.

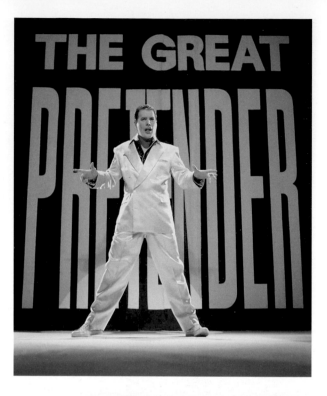

Filming *The Great Pretender* video
in 1987. Freddie later confessed,
"I am the great pretender!" so
what more perfect cover version
could there be for him?

When a Queen audience threw plastic disposable razors onto the concert
stage in 1980 (a good-humoured protest), Freddie asked them if he should
keep his moustache or lose it. "Lose it!" they jeered. "Fuck off! I'm keeping
it!" came the retort, in a flash. Freddie did so willingly, however, for *The
Great Pretender* video seven years on.

"*Barcelona* (the song and the album) was an example of the high musical talent of Freddie. He was not only a popular singer, he was a musician that could sit at the piano and compose for me. He discovered a new way to bring music together. He was the first and only person that has done this." This was Montserrat Caballé's recollection of one of popular music's most unlikely and astonishing collaborations.

From the beginning of the recording of the *Barcelona* album, in April 1987, throughout the rest of his life, Freddie shared a special friendship with Montserrat. His affection for her shows in this warm portrait taken during the photo session for their album.

Two friends at work... or at least discussing the work ahead; Freddie and the Super Diva (as he once referred to her) in conversation about... who knows what? Freddie later confessed that Montserrat often teased him during their recording sessions, and perhaps this one was on those occasions.

Oscar Mercury, 1986.
Not a lot of people know this…
but Freddie once wrote a song
called *Delilah* about his cat, for
the 1991 *Innuendo* album. He
really did love his feline pets every
bit as much as it seems.

In 1985 Freddie dedicated his first solo album, *Mr Bad Guy*, not to his
mother, father, sister, or Queen fellows, but thus:- "This album is dedicated
to my cat Jerry – also Tom, Oscar and Tiffany, and all the cat lovers across
the universe – screw everybody else."
This adored companion is Tiffany, 1986.

With Liza Minnelli, who Freddie had admired for many years and
frequently cited as an influence, at Queen's 20th Anniversary Party,
Groucho's Club, Soho, February 18th 1990. And with fellow musician and
songwriter George Michael at the same event. This was one of Freddie's
last public appearances.

Freddie with his best friend
Mary Austin at his 38th birthday
party - Xenon Club, Piccadilly,
September 5th 1984.

With Mary again at his 39th birthday celebrations –
the Black and White Drag Ball, at Hendersons Club,
Munich, September 5th 1985.

Sometimes when I'm alone at night I imagine that when I'm 50 I'll creep into Garden Lodge, as my refuge, and then start making it a home. When I'm old and grey and when everything is finished and I can't wear the same costumes and jig around on stage any more, not quite yet, I have something to fall back on, and that's this wonderful house. In the meantime I like outraging people with my music.

Chapter sixteen

FAME AND FORTUNE...

"I like to be surrounded by splendid things. I want to
lead the Victorian life, surrounded by exquisite clutter."

You cannot divide success from money.

Money may be vulgar, but it's wonderful. I cope with wealth very well, actually – I spend, spend, spend. Well, what's money for if not to spend? I spend it like it's nothing. I have lots of money yes, but I honestly couldn't tell you what my bank balance is. I'm conditioned that way. I'll just go out and spend it. I'm not one of those who stuffs his money under the mattress and counts it every night. I'm not like some of those stars who are obsessed with counting their pennies. I know several people who do a show then rush home to count what they have, but not me. I don't give a damn about money. I just think it's for spending.

I'm the one member of the band for whom money isn't very endearing. I'm the one who spends it straight off. It just goes – on clothes and the nice things I like to have around me.

All I wanted from life was to make lots of money and spend it. I always knew I would be a star, and now the rest of the world seems to agree with me. But, because I'm successful and have a lot of money, a lot of greedy people prey on me. But that's something I've learnt to deal with. The higher I climb the ladder, the bigger the barrier becomes around me. The more I open up the more I get hurt.

At one point, two or three years after we began, we nearly disbanded. We felt it wasn't working, there were too many sharks in the business and it was all getting too much for us. But something inside us kept us going and we learned from our experiences, good and bad. We didn't make any money until the fourth album, *A Night At The Opera*. Most of our income was consumed by litigation and things like that.

Once you start making big money, everyone wants a piece of the action. All the leeches move in and they will suck you dry if you give them half a chance. Money attracts all kinds of wrong people. It's true, money does always seems to be at the root of all evil. Success can bring problems you have never really bargained for, ones you think can never exist.

You have to watch everyone who works for you and if they seem to be taking you for a ride, you have to weed them out fast. You can't afford to let anyone get away with anything. I can smell a rat. It's instinctive. I can smell them out!

Dear oh dear, there have been some bad apples over the years. I don't hold a grudge, really – it's just trivia. I was shocked at certain things, and by particular people in the past. I was fucking mad about some things, but I mean what can you do? The way I see it, I think that kind of thing is going to make me stronger. I just think it might make me a harder person. I see it as something I have to overcome. It's part of my life. This is it! This is part of what my lifestyle is. I take it in my stride.

Sometimes it's all about awareness and acceptance. I mean sometimes I don't mind it if I know that I'm being taken for a ride, that way it's fine. It's when I *don't* know that I've been made a chump, that's the difference. There are many times when I've been taken for a ride knowing fully well, but I've given them enough rope to hang themselves.

You'd be surprised how slippery people can be. A few times when people have got through to me they've betrayed my trust. I built up a barrier, a feeling that anybody wanting any sort of involvement with us was bound to rip us off in some way. It gave me a very cold exterior.

The more money one makes, the more miserable one can become. It's very true that success changes you, but you have to change to survive it. I used to hang around the market in Kensington, I spent a lot of time there, and now when I go down there I know that if I don't stop and talk to everybody, they'll be hurt – whereas before I could just say hello as I passed. If I don't stop now they just say, "Oh, he thinks he's a star now."

I still drink with a lot of my friends in the pub, but sometimes I'm aware of being taken for a ride. I don't mind sometimes, but things happen like I come in and buy the drinks and people that have been drinking halves of bitter suddenly ask for Southern Comforts. I understand it. It's for similar reasons that you seem to change outwardly. You have to learn to survive the pressure that success places on you, and for that reason people that don't realise all those things think you've changed for the worse.

My object in life is to make a lot of money and spend it, though these days I tend to spend it before I make it! There is such a lot of money to be made out there. I adore spending it. I just love being lavish and extravagant. It's such fun. I'm hopeless with money. Life's too short to sit back and consider those things all the time. I'm a rock star, I'm very rich, I can buy anything that I like – including you!

I never carry money around, just like the real Queen. If I fancy something in a shop I always ask someone on our staff to buy it.

I love shopping and I love going to auctions and buying antiques at Sotheby's and Christie's. The one thing I would really miss if I left Britain would be Sotheby's. All my money goes there. Actually, that's what I've been interested in for a long while. And now that I've got a little bit of money to throw around, I thought I might as well go and spend it. So I went to Sotheby's the other day and got a few paintings. The dealers weren't pleased at all!

I love Harrods, too. And Cartier, Asprey, Christie's. The Japanese call it crazy shopping. I walk around like the Pied Piper with hordes of people following me. I'd go with the wife of the promoter to a department store left open for me after hours. All these assistants standing there and the place is entirely empty, except for me!

I like to be surrounded by splendid things. I want to lead the Victorian life, surrounded by exquisite clutter. I've got lots of junk as well, which doesn't have any value – which I love. It would be so boring if I only went out and said, "Oh, that's going to be a lovely investment."

I bought my house in London that I'd only seen in photographs. I know that's absurd, but I had no time to go house-hunting. I needed a place to move my furniture and clothes to. I have had this house for four years now. It is quite exquisite and gorgeous. People are still working on it – putting up all kinds of elaborate shit. At this rate I will probably move in when I am old and grey.

I'm trailing over my Lalique and Galle vases – I'm up to my ears now. It's getting really silly. I mean, a lot of people used to say my house was like a museum, but now I'm beginning to agree with them. It's getting very silly.

I love those stories about Elton, when he had that problem where people were staying at his home at the weekends, in his spare rooms, and they'd look under the bed and there would be Rembrandts and other such masters. It's true. With me, it's my Japanese prints that are just getting ridiculous.

People are saying, "What are you doing? You've got this massive great thing and it's costing so much money. Aren't you worried?" I've got my accountants and lawyers all brow-beating me saying it's the wrong thing to do, it's a waste of money, and this and that. Fuck that!

I want to do it properly. So maybe money-wise it's not a very good thing to do, but I'm going to do what I feel I want to do at the time – whatever my mind says, whatever my heart tells me to do.

I love it. It's all part of my nature. I thrive on it. I ride on it. I am not afraid to spend my money. Sometimes I could go to Cartier's, the jewellers, and buy up the whole shop. Often my sprees begin just like a woman buying herself a new hat to cheer herself up. Some days, when I'm really fed-up, I just want to lose myself in my money. I work up a storm and just spend and spend. Then I get back home and think, "Oh God! What have I bought?" But it's never a waste. I get an awful lot of pleasure out of giving presents.

I love buying gifts for people. That's the biggest thrill. I find that's the biggest fun. I don't like hogging it all. Money may not be able to buy happiness, but it can damn well give it! I'm not afraid to squander it in terms of giving it to other people. Yesterday I went shopping at Cartier's in London. But then I realised they were closing at lunchtime. So I rang up to see if they could leave it open for me and they actually did. So all the shutters were down and I went along there. I felt like Zsa Zsa Gabor. It was really very nice of them. I bought lots of junk from Cartier – but nothing for myself.

The bit of happiness I *can* create, is with my money. Okay, money can't buy happiness, it's true – I've written a song called *Money Can't Buy Happiness*, by the way – but depending on who you are, you can force yourself sometimes. When I buy people presents I think I love it far more than maybe they do. I love to do that kind of thing.

Having said all that… I buy a lot of shitty things for a lot of people too. The worst thing is, I get them back a few years later!

I bought somebody a car the other day. It was in the German press as well. The funny thing is that it was meant to be my car as well, but he's driving it. Suddenly I hear in the papers that I've bought a 500 Mercedes SEC. I thought, "My dear, come on!" If I wanted to give a car away, I would do that, but that's the way it happens. So he thinks it's *his* car now. It's not correct.

My favourite car, by the way, is a Rolls Royce – every time. You can't beat them for style and comfort.

Money hasn't spoiled me. I know it sounds very corny, but it's true. Buying people little things is so nice to do. Those little moments make their day; a little gift, a gesture, a nuance, just a little treasure. It means far more than somebody buying you Big Ben, or something. People treasure the *little* things.

I'll tell you a good example. The other day Mary gave me a wonderful present that I haven't seen before. It's something that nobody else would think of, and it might be totally useless for you, but it's something from somebody who cares and that's what matters. She gave me this little gift that she went out of her way to arrange. It was the newspaper of the day that I was born – so you can actually read about what was going on when you were born. It was *The Times*, September 5th, 1946. And she also got me 1846, which was wonderful. I thought that was a lovely little treat – just a little something. There's reams and reams of paper and it was wonderful. She said, "This'll keep you busy, dear. You can read it while you're on the throne." I like to read when I'm having a crap!

The 1846 edition was so interesting. It was during the days of cholera. Suddenly there was an epidemic in India, and it was during the Raj and the East India Company, and all that stuff. About 100 English people in India got cholera, including 858 sepoys. Wonderful, isn't it? Who knows what *sepoys* are, but I mean it gave me great joy... just a newspaper.

I think it is totally farcical to assume that people who have money don't need little gestures like that – like everybody else does. I think there might be a lot of people who just pooh-pooh that kind of stuff, but they must be very boring types.

Some people think that you have all this money so, "What can I possibly get you as a present? You have everything, so I can't buy you anything," I think that's a cop-out. There are tons of things I need. I hate all those excuses. They think they can't give you something that doesn't cost much because it's going to be beneath you, but that's absolute crap.

I could never be a kept person. Never! Never ever! It's just not in me. It would be like rubbing a cat up the wrong way. I could never be that. Everybody would like to be kept, but I think my ultimate ambition is for somebody really wealthy, somebody rich and famous, to come up to me and say, "It would be lovely to *keep* you," just for somebody to actually say that to me. And then I can say, "No, fuck off!"

At the same time, there are a lot of people the other way. I don't like keeping people either. I don't like to be on the other side, if you know what I mean. This might sound like I'm being a hypocrite but I'm not, I like a relationship to work on an even basis, believe it or not.

I can live without fame quite easily. My lifestyle doesn't suddenly stop because fame might end. If all my money ended tomorrow I would still be the same person. I'd still go about the same way, like I had lots of money, because that's what I used to do before. With or without money, I seem to do it. That's the only way to do it. I like living life to the full. That's my nature, and I'm just not going to conform or listen to people about how I should react. I do what I want to do. That's something inbred, that's part of me. I've always been like this. Success does help, it makes it easier to be outrageous or whatever, but it's not the be all and end all. In the early days, when I had hardly anything, I'd save for two weeks and then blow it all in a day so that I could have a blast of fun. I'll always walk round like a Persian Popinjay and no-one's going to stop me. Nobody tells me what to do.

I've been going on wild spending sprees lately. I've been told to cool down because the taxman will be coming to take a large sum away. I've spent in the region of £100,000 over the last three years. I don't like life too easy, so if I keep spending a lot then, I'll have to keep earning it. That's how I push myself.

I can spend small fortunes in just a couple of hours, but it's money well spent. I always want to look good because the people who make you a so-called star in this business are entitled to see you always looking like a star. I'm not into business at all. I'm hopeless with money. I don't believe in putting money in the bank. It's for using, not hoarding. I simply spend what I've got. I guess I've always lived the glamorous life of a star. It's nothing new. I used to spend down to the last dime, and now I've got money, I'll keep spending.

I've got a few good friends, a big house, and I can go wherever I want, whenever I want. But the more money you make the more miserable you get. It just so happens that I have a lot of money.

I make sure I get most of it and I spend it. I take most of it, dears. I take most of it because I write all the hits. Now *that's* controversial. When I say that, I'm just being logical. If you write the hits you make the money.

Basically, the money is divided into quarters; it's the four of us. It goes down that way. But if you want to get into the nitty-gritty, it's all to do with publishing. The writer makes more money because if he writes he gets the publishing royalties. So, if an album consists of say ten songs and Brian and I have written four each, and Roger and John have written one, then of course Brian and I will make more money. It's just down to the mechanicals.

Of course we're in it for the money, and I'm not afraid to say that. We love the money. Anybody who tells you differently is talking out of their arse – they really are. Money is part of it, yes, but of course it's for the glory too. It would be quite easy for me to give up right now, because I have all I need, but to be serious, it's not just for the money, it's the longevity too.

I know nothing else. To me this is quite a normal life. It's like winning the pools, except I win the pools every day. I've worked very hard for the money. Nobody gave it to me. I worked for all these things. I worked for it and I've paid for it. To have my wonderful Japanese garden with all the koi carp, recently bought at such expense, I love it. Anybody who likes koi, if they had the money, would buy it, so why not me?

I think I've earned my keep. I worked hard for what I've got and I value that more than anything. I hate freebies. I'm not into buckshee. I like to feel that what I've got is through my own doing.

I don't want my money to rule me, but that doesn't mean I'm a pushover. You see, that's the difference. Money doesn't control me. All I need is to honestly be able to say to myself that I'm still trying and still enjoying the whole business of singing in Queen.

I don't think I could do anything else. I know it sounds awful, but I'm so full of self-confidence, something somewhere is always going to come off for me. I'm just going to make sure that I keep what I have.

I think if I lost what I have now it would be a disaster. But it wouldn't stop me, I would cope. I wouldn't let having no money stop me having a good time. I could be penniless tomorrow and if I lost everything tomorrow, I'd claw my way back to the top somehow.

The only real friend I've had is Mary. She will inherit the bulk of my fortune. What better person to leave it to when I go? Of course, my parents are in my Will, and so are my cats, but the vast bulk of it will go to Mary. If I dropped dead tomorrow, she's the one person I know who could cope with my vast wealth. She's in charge of all my money and possessions; the chauffeurs, maids, gardeners, accountants and lawyers. All I have to do is throw my carcass around on stage.

No-one else will get a penny – except for my cats Oscar and Tiffany. Other than that, I'm not giving any of my stuff away when I'm dead. I'm going to hoard it. I want to be buried with all my stuff. Anybody who wants it, can come with me. There'll be lots of room!

Chapter seventeen

...AND EVERYTHING THAT GOES WITH IT

"I don't care what journalists say.
What do they know? Fuck them if they just don't get it!"

In terms of the press, I'm a very hated person. But I hate the press as well, so that goes both ways.

I think I've learned to live with it after all these years. I'd be a liar to say I'm not hurt by criticism because everybody is. Of course I want everybody to say I'm wonderful and that they like my songs, and I don't mind genuine well thought out criticism, but of course you're going to get people who review our albums without even listening to them, and things like that. That's the way of the world. I used to get really mad and start tearing my hair out, but I don't have sleepless nights any more. I learned to live with it. It needs a strong-willed person to survive in this industry. You have to be astute and strong. You have to be a hard-faced bitch.

I've never let the press worry me. In the early days you think about it, you go out and buy the papers and make sure you're in it, but now it's a completely different set-up because it's just your music you worry about. Basically what you worry about is the people that buy your products – that's who keeps us going.

I don't give a damn about critics, to be honest. The backing of the press is important only at the beginning of a career as a rock musician. When success arrives, it's the fans who decide on whether it's to be, or not to be. They can write what they want. You'd be surprised how much of it is exaggerated and blown up by the press just to make good copy. I would give them a bit of spice, and they would add all the trimmings. I wish I didn't talk so much to people because the more I find out, the more I realise how cruel it can be. My lifestyle and this very precocious nature was blown out of all proportion. But the media created a lot more than I could give. I was prepared to live with it, and it was up to me to make sure I had one foot firmly on the ground. I feel I have. What's more important to me is the public. Critics don't buy my records, they don't give me the money, so until the public stop buying my records I don't have to think about it.

Anybody that's successful for long has to take a little bit of flak. It makes them better. You can't be a goody-two-shoes forever. I can't bear the fact there are a few musicians who think they are *so* wonderful. I think that's terrible. We all have our ups and downs, we all have our limitations, and we all know there are certain things you can't do. But I don't want some arsehole critic telling me that. I would rather have a man-to-man talk with a real musician, who can tell me I'm doing certain things wrong.

I think it would be a very stupid person who is in this position to think that nothing derogatory is ever going to come out about them. That would be very silly. I always knew there were going to be exposés. It just depends how horrible they are, of course. I think most of us know that is always on the sideline. You always know. It's something we live with.

It's dreadful. I think what I'm saying is that I knew there were going to be people who would suddenly do me wrong – those who say, "I'm going to dish the dirt on him!" I always knew there was going to be somebody in the camp to do it one day. Actually, I was amazed it didn't happen sooner. I won't name names, but I've been terribly betrayed in the past. It's something you have to live with and then in the end if you're clever enough it just makes you stronger.

I think it's an element of human nature, too, so I put it down to that. It's a trait, a characteristic that most of us have. It's a human thing.

There are lots of stories where people take exposés to the media about successful people, because nobody wants to read about ordinary Mary Potts, and her depressing life, poor girl! It doesn't make for very good reading. But somebody of status, any kind of celebrity, they know it sells papers.

I'm the first to accept fair criticism, and I think it would be wrong if all we got were good reviews, but it's when you get unfair, dishonest reviews, where people haven't done their homework, that I get annoyed. I just tear reviews like that up.

To be frank I'm not that keen on the British music press, as they've been pretty unfair to us. I get annoyed when up-and-coming journalists put themselves above the artists. They've certainly been under a misconception about us. We've been called a 'supermarket hype'. But if you see us up on a stage, that's what we're all about. We are basically a rock band. All the lights and paraphernalia are only there to enhance what we do. I think we're good writers, and we want to play good music, no matter how much of a slagging we get. The music is the most important factor.

We did our first headline tour and the buzz got around, without any support from the media. I suppose they like to find their own bands, and we were too quick for them.

I don't take much notice, to be honest. They can say what they like. It's not constructive at all. The American press do their homework and the kind of questions they ask you makes much better copy anyway. They ask more relevant things, I feel. You can tell that they've done their homework because they ask you very penetrating questions – which I don't mind – because then you know they have some substance – what they write about has much more bearing. But over here, in England, it's all, "Why have you stopped wearing black fingernails Freddie Mercury?" Then it's the review of the album, and they haven't a clue anyway.

In this country, to gain any sort of respect over a given period seems very difficult, to say the least. The papers like to feel they have you in their grasp. Well, we slipped out of their grasp.

The Americans don't have the same kind of prejudices. If they can do it, why can't people over here? They're too narrow-minded here. They are arrogant sods that just don't want to learn. They don't want to be told anything. They feel that they know it all before it's even happened.

We're not just an average rock group. We did things that people least expected, not for the sake of just doing them, but because it was the phase we were going through. Some people used to think that all we used to do was copy rock and that we could only do one sort of style. I felt sorry for certain journalists who were very narrow-minded and thought that way, because all they had to do was delve a bit deeper and do a bit more of their homework to have found out what the band was really all about.

It could be that we got people's backs up because it seemed that we broke through so fast. We gained popularity quicker than most bands and we were talked about more than most other bands, so it was inevitable. One minute nobody had heard of us, next minute we were top of the bill. But it didn't happen like that, of course. We kind of crept up on the press boys. Really, they like to take the credit for discovering new bands in advance of public interest, but in our case we were there before they latched on.

From the very beginning, as far as the music press is concerned, they like to put up and coming bands into a particular bag, to what they think you should be. We were disliked by them in the early days because they couldn't put their finger on us. That was the case with Zeppelin as well. We just rebelled and wanted to do what we thought was right, and not go along with what they were saying. Since the early stages there's been this fracas. Now it's the standard thing – it's just the norm. It doesn't worry me at all. It was more frustrating in the early days when the press were not very favourable towards us. I got very depressed as far as Britain was concerned, but now I think we've learned to live with it. We've been living with that kind of thing for years.

My private life is private, and okay little bits of it sneak out, and I can come up with outrageous quotes, and that's as far as I go. There are always going to be people in the press after you – all out to get you.

Recently I was completely misquoted in a newspaper article again. From the beginning the press have always written whatever they wanted about Queen, and they can get away with it. The woman who wrote that last story wanted a total scoop from me but didn't get anything. I said, "What do you want to hear... that I deal cocaine?" But for God's sake, if I want to make big confessions about my sex life, or to make a fucking crash-landing, like a tidal wave, a big splash after all these years, would I go to *The Sun*, of all papers, to do it? It wouldn't be to some rag like that. There's no fucking way I'd do that. I'm too intelligent.

It's strategy. One has to use it to one's best advantage. Darlings, if everything you read in the press about me was true, I wouldn't be sitting here talking to you today. I would be so worried about my ego. Actually, if it was all accurate, I would have burnt myself out by now, I really would have.

The media were trying to break us up almost from when we started, when we became successful. That's what the press love. I think they'd love to split Queen up. I think it's one of those done things, where you know after so many years that they are going to try. So many of them decided we needed a good slagging, just because we had the nerve to get to the top before they had given us the say-so. We'd always had confidence in what we were doing, so the press didn't really get us down. If we break up, we break up, and the press will want to be the first ones to know.

I'm getting a bit sober in my old age. Honestly, I don't think about it. I'm really not that conscious about it, not now. I don't give two shits if people slander me or talk about me. I used to get very paranoid about what people said in the early days, and I wanted to be put across in the way I felt, but now it's growing out of all proportion and you can't keep track of all that.

These days I get a bit annoyed if I'm *not* quoted in teasers or misquoted in teasers. I look forward to those days. A lot of misguided opinions can hurt because you feel that the guy hasn't got it right or done it properly, but yet people are going to read it and take it in and feel that it's accurate. That's the thing that hurts a bit. But what can you do? Sometimes you can do an interview and say certain things and then it comes out totally wrong. I feel that the bloody British press are good at that. You do an hour-long interview and then you just get a paragraph where they only take the juicy lines, and you think, "Oh dear, oh dear!" Sometimes you do an interview and then the article is published and you think, "Was I actually there for that?" because it's nothing like what you originally said. That's happened to me so many times but it's something that one has to learn to live with. I never take it that seriously. There was a time, like I said before, when I thought it was affecting me, but you must never let it get on top of you. You must just put it aside and look upon it more generally. That's the way I look at it. It's only an article!

I believe in personalities, not papers. I'm not interested in us versus the *New Musical Express*. People think that because I don't do interviews any more, I've got this thing against the press. It's not true. I don't like doing interviews because if you plonk a tape recorder in front of me I just clam up.

I think to an extent we are a sitting target in the press, because we became popular so quickly. But we spent two years putting our act together. It destroys the soul to hear that you're all 'hype', that you have no talent, and that your whole career has been contrived. I was never too keen on the British music press. They used to suggest that we didn't write our own songs… when the whole point of Queen was to be original. I don't care what the journalists say, we have achieved our own identity. What do they know? Fuck them if they just don't get it!

Chapter eighteen

STAYING POWER

"There will come a time when we do have to call it a day,
when I can't run around on stage because it will look ridiculous,
but none of us has any intention of leaving.
It would be cowardice to stop now."

Staying successful at our level is hard. When you've tasted success as beautifully as I have, you don't want to let go in a hurry.

The hardest thing after all these years is to maintain the level of success that you've achieved. No group can afford to get in a rut. They must be ready to change with, or even ahead of, the times, if they are to remain successful.

I think we feel that our success is justified because we have worked hard. I think these are our just rewards. I've worked fucking hard, and I still am.

It's very difficult, especially after so long, to come up with totally outrageous and original ideas. I want to do different things. I don't want to keep to the same formula over and over again, otherwise you just go insane. I don't want to become stale. I want to be creative.

People expect that much more from you when you're successful, but in a way you're only as good as your last album. I think the public can be very fickle, but in one way I like that. I think they will gauge you by what you did last, and if you had a humongous hit, you've got to try and fight that and better it.

I don't know what the answer is. You just have to try to do your best. You really can't rest on your laurels – it's not the done thing. We can hide behind what we've done before, that's quite easy, but none of us want to do that.

That's always at the back of your mind. The only way to find out is to make an album and see how it goes. To be honest you're always worrying about that and if you've been away for a while, no matter how big or successful you are, you always have that at the back of your mind, that they might have forgotten you, or they probably think you're dead or broken up, or whatever. I think now they know we're still happening.

We want to do interesting songs constantly. The day we try and do something that isn't interesting for us will be the day that we're a dead group. We will stick to our guns, and if we're worth anything, we will live on. If we were doing something that the media expected us to do, that certainly would be a downward step. At the moment we're happy because we're doing what we feel is right. We've never catered to the media and we never will.

We were confident about our music and we wanted to put it across properly. And if we found that we'd come to a stage where we'd hit a compromise, we wouldn't do it. There would be cases where we'd cut off our nose to spite our face, but I think it's worked in the long run, because the truth and what we believed in came across. It doesn't work in all cases, always, but in our case it has. Am I talking a load of shit?

There's always got to be that challenge to get further. That's why when people say, "What are you going to do now that you've hit your peak?" I say, "Bullshit! We haven't hit our peak yet." I hate admitting to myself that we've reached our peak, you know, because after that the only way is down. I think when you go all the way up, the only place left is to come down. When you're climbing the escalator of success, you keep treading at the top because you don't want to go down. That's a hard thing.

The biggest challenge is trying to keep the band going, when everybody says it's breaking up. Everybody thinks the band is going to break up. There came a point where I, we, were all getting very despondent and we wanted to do different things. And when you have that in your bloodstream, as it were, the slightest thing that happens, or that's said… you just need the slightest excuse to actually break up the band.

How much higher can you go? You have to find different things to do. You say, "Okay, there's this little gap that's left and we have to sort of push ourselves in this direction.

You've got to have nerves of steel to survive the pace. When you have success it becomes really difficult, because then you really learn the things behind the business. You find out the real baddies. When you start out you don't know anything about it. You have to be very strong and sift them out. Anyone who is successful will always be burned once or twice.

There's no such thing as an easy climb to success – or an escalator to the top. There's always going to be a competitive field. Everything now is just growing and growing in rock music, more so than ever.

If there was a book of rules everybody would buy it and everyone would be churning out the same old trash.

We knew when we embarked, as it were, when we launched ourselves, when we took the plunge, that it was going to be hard slog all the way and we were prepared to take that. If we didn't have that foresight in the early days we would have come a cropper.

There's only so much you can rely on in terms of ready-made acceptance. Loyalty from your fan-base is one thing, but you can't expect, just because you've had one hit, that it'll go on. You have to keep coming up with the goods. If you can't come up with the goods when it's needed, then forget it. You can't live on your past and I can't live on *Bohemian Rhapsody* all the time, because that's a totally different generation. You cannot remain constant. You must change all the time.

It gets harder all the time. In terms of competition, there are lots of wonderful new bands and they seem to come up with newer ideas and they

147

are fresh – and there is newer technology. It's very hard. You've got to be very aware, and I feel as if I'm always on my toes. I like to see what the new people are doing because it's quite easy to say, "Oh, after ten years of success, we can do the same old thing." I hate doing the same thing again. I like to see what's happening now and incorporate all these thoughts into Queen. I'm very aware of that and it keeps me going. My interests are in what's going on now. It's a kind of research. I go to all the ballets and I go to all the musicals to find out what's happening. I want to do interesting things and things that I haven't done before.

You can become blasé after you've had a lot of success for a long time. It's quite easy to say, "Oh yes, we're the greatest!' but I really don't think we're that kind of group. We make our own challenges. It's quite easy to think that because you did it ten years ago, you can do the same old thing again. I hate repeating the same formulas again.

There are so many people now that I know who are bursting with talent, but they just haven't got the right timing or the right environment to improve themselves, and that can be very frustrating. We are in a very lucky position at the moment but even then one cannot just sit back and rest on ones laurels.

After all these years of playing together, sometimes we can get bored of each other, to be honest, and sometimes you want to do something other than just Queen, Queen, Queen. I like Queen very much, but I want to do something different otherwise I'll get too damn old and be in a wheelchair, and it'll be too late for anything else.

We can't live as a quartet *all* the time, so you feel like every time you make a move it's like a four-headed gorgon, or something. Do you know what I mean? I like to feel that I'm an individual. That break is very hard to achieve. It's horrible to just be thought of as one quarter of some entity.

At one point, two or three years after we began, we nearly disbanded. We felt it wasn't working, there were too many sharks in the business and it was all getting too much for us. But something inside us kept us going and we learned from our experiences, good and bad.

There were times where I thought I should call it a day, and there will come a time when we do have to call it a day, when I can't run around on stage in a leotard because it will look ridiculous, and it's not very becoming, but none of us has any intention of leaving. It would be cowardice to stop now. The chemistry has worked for us, so why kill the goose that lays the golden egg?

I think when it gets hectic, when we do an album and we start to get on each other's nerves, and it's a solid work-out, it's then you start thinking, "Is it really worth it after all these years? Why don't we just go our separate ways and enjoy it?" I think about these things. So do the rest of them.

It gets very petty after a while. Everything. Songs, the music, the musical aspects. It's all to do with money, so we might as well be open about it. A lot of the time it's about how each musician is displayed on an album, so like if I had more songs than somebody else, it would make them a lesser musician. That's how near the mark it can get. I'm always trying to make it very diplomatic, so I just said, "Okay, no matter what it is, we all have even songs from now on."

After all these years you don't want it to be such a fight to get anything done. You've already done that thing, and I think most of it should be fun – like live recording should be fun.

I think we are four people that in the end need that kind of thing, even though we don't like it. If it were too easy, we would lose interest. So, we think, "Oh my God! We'd better go back in and carry on fighting." I suppose that's the way I am.

The reason we're successful, darlings? My overall charisma of course! Seriously though, I think the reason we've stayed together so long is because none of us wants to leave. If you leave it's like you're being a coward. As long as the people still buy the music then it's okay.

After all these years, all that time, if you're still together you like each other instinctively. You don't have to think about spending social time together, which we hardly ever do. Basically we only come together when there is music. Basically it's a job. We've done a lot together and now all we're doing is staying together to make music, which is what we were initially there to do.

I think longevity is a very important part of this business. After the first few years you have to think about how you're going to adapt to your role in life, within this circle, because this becomes your life. You have to live and breathe it. That's the way I think about it.

It's a survival test. Of course we could all just go away and say ok we've had enough, and live happily ever after, but that's not what we're in for. We're in it to make music. This is the thing that interests me most.

We are very busy and I have had offers to do other bits, but I haven't done that because basically I feel that there is so much more to do within the Queen format. I wouldn't want to do anything else because I would be forsaking the other ideas.

I couldn't think beyond Queen at the moment. We are riding on the crest of a wave. I feel like we are a volcano that's really going to erupt. There is so much more to Queen and I feel that over the next few years we are going to take it much further.

If I felt the band wasn't going any place, it would have been disbanded. But I think we've come a long way. And I've just got this go-ahead nature. It needs a combination of arrogance and confidence. People can *still* relate to me and the band. Why do you think Hollywood was so successful? It's decadence and things like that. It's the kind of lifestyle I've grown up with. We will stick to our guns, and if we're worth anything we will live on.

The rumours that Queen are splitting up are always doing the rounds. Some people just seem to want us to break up. Heaven knows why. Yes, there are a lot of tensions and stresses in the band, and sometimes we have the most almighty rows, but they just clear the air. It isn't true to say we *always* row. Let's just say there's degree of tension which often pushes us into sticky situations. But once we've got down to the business of making music, everything else is forgotten. Besides, I would rather we had the occasional almighty blow-up than days of sulking and not speaking to one another, which is so counter-productive.

The rows can be fierce, but at least they iron out any problems and each of us knows where he stands. We don't hate each other. If we did, it would be a different matter, but the reverse is true. Our blow-outs happen because we become jaded. It can be draining and uninspiring working as hard as we do, and you constantly have to be on your guard to stop things becoming monotonous. There was a time, for instance, when all our tours seemed to be in the winter, and I wanted to break that. I just thought, "For fuck's sake, let's do a summer tour. Let's do something different."

The break-up rumours are always around. Either your egos take you away from all that and you break up, or it brings you closer together. At the moment we are very much together."

I think we've got to a stage where we will do whatever we want. I think that is the best way of doing it. I hate to conform and pander to even public tastes – or as far as record company people are concerned. In fact, I was thinking about this a couple of days ago and I thought, "My god, we were outrageous and innovative in the days of *Bohemian Rhapsody*, and that's why it worked. But for us to start pandering to people's tastes now, saying this is what they want so give it to them, would be such a back-lash.

So we're going to do things against the grain, against people's ideas of whatever they like or expect us to do. We're not afraid of the fact that we're doing those things. We don't jump on bandwagons or do whatever is modern. No, we do it with the Queen stamp on everything. But we're aware, we're not stupid. We don't just churn out the same stuff that we did like five or six years ago. We're in tune to what's going on and that's the way I like to live.

I love the challenge and I love doing things that are not part of the mainstream. Sometimes if that works it works in a very big way, or else it can be a very big flop, but I'm willing to take that risk.

I remember we had an album called *Hot Space* which died a death in America and everybody said, "Oh yes, Queen took a big risk, but failed, so now they'll know that that's *not* what they should do." No, that doesn't happen. If that's what I want to do again, I'll do it.

I think we've just grown so used to each other by now, it's just instinct that keeps us going. There's no big bond. Musically we still respect each other.

It's just fate. It's an ingredient that we have, a chemistry, and it's a combination that seems to have worked for us. That doesn't mean we don't have egos, we all have terrible egos, so there's always been talk of breaking up. There's been lots of very bad moods and there's always been somebody or other, one of us, saying, "I want to call it a day." But I think things seem to be working out right. There's no pill that we're taking to keep together, you can't put a finger on it.

At this point, I'm quite amazed that we still keep going and that people are still buying our records, and people still think of us as a unit to be reckoned with. After all these years that is quite something. The Stones are doing it after 27 albums, so I suppose we've still got something.

I'm dumbfounded that we've stayed together all these years. All the other bands have always broken up or changed personnel, but we are about the only four grande dames that have actually stuck together. We all have our ego problems, but we never let it get too much. Long may we reign!

We went a bit overboard sometimes, but that's the way Queen is. In certain areas we always feel that we want to go overboard. It's what keeps us going really.

It's time for some stocktaking. We've all become businessmen, even though it's against our better judgment. It's something that always happens if you get successful. Being a musician is not just cutting discs, unfortunately. I wish it were. We've all got companies now, some connected to music, others not – lots of other fingers in other pies. We must take some time off to get things in perspective or things will start to go wrong.

This is the best industry to be in because you can get rich and have a wonderful time, but it's very hard work. I'm very happy doing this. If I weren't I'd give it up. It's not the money any more. I'm still hungry to do things. This is what I'm best at.

If anyone left, any one of the four, that would be the end of Queen. We are four equal, interwoven parts. And the others just couldn't function the same without each quarter.

We are four. It's a strong quartet. We are going to stay together until we fucking well die. It's got to the point where we're actually too old to break up now.

After Live Aid, and our 1986 tour breaking all box-office records in certain places, that's sort of gave us even more of an impetus to carry on. So why leave now? What the hell am I going to do anyway? Oh, here we go again. I've nothing else to do. I could become a gardener, actually. So many things happen in my garden. I could become a Japanese landscape gardener.

We are going to take a little rest, a well earned break – I hope anyway. I think if we leave it too long then we will disperse and go our separate ways. I think the time is right to strike while the iron's hot.

We shouldn't let ourselves go into different areas too far away from each other, so I've told them it's something we should actually think about. That way, at least we know we have that in the back of our heads, so we don't go rushing around doing solo projects so far beyond, that we can't come back.

I'm a man of moods, dears, so after that Magic tour I suddenly thought that everything was going so well that I got a sort of new-found force. Suddenly, there was more left in Queen. We really want to stay together.

I think we know now instinctively what each other wants. It's like a job, as I say. You come together, do a gig, then we go our separate ways. We have four limousines waiting after each show and we just go wherever we want.

If we ever think we are on a decline, we'll just give it up. No-one is ever going to tell me I've had my day, had my innings, now do something else.

I admire people who can do that – who actually feel it's not quite happening, that they've given it their best, and now it's time to just try something else. But it has to be *you*. It has to be you in the end, eventually... no matter what. You could have numerous people coming up saying that, but in the end the realisation has to come from you. You have to accept the fact that it's now over and you've done enough. That has to happen one day.

That's why I think – and I may be overstepping the mark – someone like Nureyev is virtually reaching that point where a lot of people are saying that he's very old, for a dancer, and he can't recreate the amazing roles that he used to. But he's still a good fighting horse, you know, and he's doing it. There will come a point where he has to say to himself, "I've had enough." That's why he's getting into directing now and things like that. He says that he feels he has a couple of years left and he's going to give it his all, and then he's going to leave.

Over time, if you have remained successful, you get that following of people that grew up with you. They keep up with you and will accept anything you do – that's what a staunch fan is, as far as I'm concerned. They will believe in what you do. In terms of Queen, we just chop and change so much, and a stoic fan will readily accept whatever we come up with next.

I think we have a hardcore of fans. After all, it's really only a game... but a serious game. A lot of people have actually grown up with us, and they still like us, and also I think we've lost a lot of people. There might be fans that I speak to in the street who say, "I like your earlier stuff, but I don't like what you're doing now." But then, at the same time, there are people who come up and say they like our new stuff and don't even know what we did five or six years ago, so it sort of balances out I guess.

Queen's fans are a wide cross section, which is really good. I'd hate to think we had a specific following. It's lovely that it's that way, and I would rather it was that way than maybe with somebody like David Essex, who has a kind of straight-forward following. We seem to have very different fans depending on where you go. It's good that we don't have fans that are like hoards of lemmings – although you do get the occasional kamikaze fan that once they've made their mind up to get you, then they are going to get you. Once the kamikaze fans make up their minds to get you, there is no stopping them unless you have a kind of karate bodyguard. It literally is like a version of Hitchcock's 'The Birds' sometimes – especially in Japan with all the screaming fans that kind of want to *peck* at you, it's very surreal, it's a totally different trip. But you know audiences vary greatly in this country as well.

It could all end tomorrow. I'm not afraid of it. It's a precarious life but I think I like it that way. I like it a little risky. Okay, so I'm quite well off, but money in the bank doesn't mean anything to me. I spend it as quickly as it comes. I could be penniless tomorrow, but I wouldn't care that much. I have this survival instinct in me.

I don't get up every morning and ask myself what I'd do if Queen decided to end. I'll take it when it comes. We're as serious about our work as a lawyer. I can't predict whether we will go on, but as long as we keep breaking new ground, the fire will remain in Queen. I don't think we've reached our peak. Within the band there's still a lot left to be done. Queen is still around. We've had no disorder or any bad vibes recently. I think everybody's quite happy at the moment. The four old ladies are still rocking away!

Through anything, we will just carry on until one of us drops dead, or something, or is just replaced. I think if I suddenly left they'd have the mechanism to replace me. Not easy to replace me, huh!?

Chapter nineteen

IN THE LAP OF THE GODS

*"From now on, dressing up crazily on stage is out.
I don't think a 42-year old man should be running around
in his leotard any more. It's not very becoming."*

We have been very lucky. I didn't think we were going to last this long. I thought after five years it was all going to be over and I'd have to think of something else to do – become a charlady or something.

I'm very proud of the fact that I'm still around after all this time, that I'm still selling records, and that I'm still a force to be reckoned with. I didn't expect to be. I'm proud, and also amazed. I've still got a musical output and I'm still accepted. You hear about these people whose pots are running dry and I'm so pleased I can still come up with different things – new songs and new ideas after all this time. That to me is tops. It's the cherry on the top of the cake. It's got to the point where we are actually too old to break up now. Can you imagine forming a new band at 40? Be a bit silly wouldn't it?

We do things now in a style that is very different to anybody else. It just happened. We just do *our* thing, because that's what we really believe in. I think Queen have actually got a new lease of life. After so many years I thought people might forget about us, but it's been like a re-birth recently. I'm quite amazed. It gives you an added incentive to think that people still like you and that's what keeps you going. It's like I've said on stage... until you buggers stop buying our records, we'll still be here. If you want us, we'll be here.

It's a question of coming to recognise the fact that it might all be over one day, and the more we carry on, the nearer we are to that situation. In the back of my mind I know it obviously will end, and that it could end any day now. That's more my motivation than anything. I get more of a drive by thinking that way than anything else.

I don't want to sound like Gloria Swanson or something, but I will NOT come to the realisation that it's going to end. At the moment I feel we still have something quite worthwhile to offer – we're still just as confident as we were when we started off.

One way or another I'm going to try and make sure that I stick in the music industry because that's all I know how to do, to be honest. I've forgotten all my other trades. I couldn't go back to illustration because I've lost all contact with that world.

I would be such a boring person if I woke up every morning and thought, "God, what am I going to do if it's all over today?" I'll wait for that and if it happens then it will be spontaneous. For the life of me at the moment I don't know what I would do. But I don't think in those terms. For now it *is* happening for us, so why the hell should I think like that? That's like being negative, and I don't want to be negative. I just want to carry on and come up with fresh ideas and think about what to do next. It's like a big business thing and as long as we don't take it too seriously, we will be fine.

I'm very happy doing it. If I weren't, I'd give it up. It's not the money any more. In one way, I feel obligated to the fans. To get this far and then suddenly say, "Yes, I've made my money, that's it now!" No, that's not me. I'm going to give it my all, still. This is what I'm best at.

At this point in time I'm having a good time. Before, I was very serious and caught up in being successful and being a star, and all that, and I thought, "This is the way a star behaves." Now, I don't give a damn. I just want to do things my way, and I want to have fun doing it. If I approach everything I do in that way I think it comes out in the songs I create. Basically I've learned to calm down. I'm not as paranoid as I was before. I'm not afraid to speak out and say the things I want, or do the things I want to do. In the end, being natural and being genuine is what wins, and I hope that comes across too. I'm not worried about making mistakes. I'm too old for that.

In ten years time I certainly won't be wearing the same costumes and running around on stage. I don't know what I'll be doing then, but I know one thing... I'll still be having a good time.

I've personally had it with these bombastic lights and staging effects. From now on, dressing up crazily on stage is out. I don't think a 42-year old man should be running around in his leotard any more. It's not very becoming. At 45, 50, if people think I'm going to be running around on that stage, they're mistaken. It would be totally wrong. It'd be silly. I'm going to put our music across dressed more casually. The world has changed – people want something more direct.

The days of screaming fans and everything that goes with that are over for us. We've grown up. The people who buy our records have grown up as well. It's more sophisticated and more mature now.

We've been very successful worldwide and that's one thing I could never have foreseen, our success outside Britain. I think we've got a certain amount of recognition and respectability now, for being respectable musicians who wrote good songs. That's good enough for me.

I want to go to places I've never been. To me it's all about people. Music should go all around the world. I want to go to Russia and China and places like that, places I haven't seen, before it's too late – before I end up in a wheelchair and can't do anything. And... I'll still be wearing my same tights too! I can imagine them wheeling me on stage in a wheelchair, up to a piano, and still singing *Bohemian Rhapsody*.

If I want to try different things – walk a tightrope, live a knife-edge – and do things where if I fall completely flat on my face and do things which are harmful to my career, so what? I will.

There are a lot of things I have done in my career that maybe I shouldn't have undertaken, but you learn by your mistakes. I regret a few of them, but doesn't everybody? I think it was a wrong decision to maybe go with certain managerial options we took on in the earlier years, but then I can even look upon them and say, "Well, I'm glad, because that's how I learned."

Things like wearing tights on stage. At the time of course I was totally convinced about doing that. When I did the balletic thing and was wearing certain outfits, I remember, as usual, the media took it all out of proportion, saying, "Oh, there you are, Freddie Mercury's gonna change rock 'n' roll, bringing ballet into the pop music genre." And I think if I still had long hair and black fingernails and was wearing those things now, I would look ridiculous. I looked ridiculous then, but it worked!

When I look back on all that black nail varnish, chiffon, satin and all those props, I think, "God! What was I doing?" I used to feel a need for all that on stage. It made me feel more secure. But now I don't. I've grown up a bit. I look back on it and think, "Oh, what an arsehole!" and "What a silly girl!" Then I laugh at it. A lot of my costumes are totally embarrassing to look back on now, but I took them so seriously at the time. But I always had an element of humour too.

Nobody could take the piss out of me as much as I take the piss out of myself. I did that with all those costumes and various other things. I was thinking, "Don't take yourself so seriously." And the best way to do that is to put on a ridiculous costume and go on the stage and appear to be so serious – but just have tongue in cheek and say to yourself, "As long as *you* know, it's ok." I loved it. It was wonderful.

In my day, as it were, that was the thing – glam rock was in. We just went for that – the clothes and glamour and the whole image. If I hadn't changed, I tell you I wouldn't be here today.

I don't regret too many decisions I made. I look upon some of the things I did with disgust and of course think, "My God, how could I have done that?" but I must say, over all, I will stand by most of the decisions I've taken.

159

I've had upheavals and I've had immense problems, but I've had a wonderful time and I have no regrets. Oh dear, I sound like Edith Piaf!

I can't retire. What else would I do? It's a very funny thing. I'm very happy with what I've achieved. I've got where I want to be. I have enough money, I have success and adulation. What more do I want? I'm just a musical prostitute my dears!

I've earned my keep, to be honest. I worked hard for what I've got. I've worked hard for the money. Nobody's given it to me. I've earned it and it's mine to do what I want with. I look back and I say to myself, "Well done my dear. Good luck to you. You did it yourself."

If I had to do it all again? Yes. Why not? I might do some of it slightly differently. I have no regrets.

Chapter twenty

TAKING MY RIDE WITH DESTINY

*"I don't expect to make old bones, and what's more I don't really care.
I certainly don't have any aspirations to live to 70.
It would be so boring. I will be dead and gone long before that."*

Some people can take second best, but I can't. I look upon it as a defeat. If you've got the taste of being number one, then number two isn't good enough.

What I'm doing right now is what interests me most and I'm very happy that people buy my records and that they like me. I don't want to just give it up. When my legs give out, I'll be happy to just sit around in bandages, knitting socks for sailors! The only way I'm going to stop is if people stop buying my records. As long as the people are buying the music, then it's ok. When they stop buying our records I'll say goodbye and do something else – become a strip artist or go into painting or something.

I'll carry on as long as I write music and people want to buy it. That's important to me, but it's not the be all and end all. I'm not going to be of those old hams that keep going and going. I'd rather leave it at the top and do something else.

I want to carry on doing what I am doing, but there's a price to pay and I'm quite prepared to pay it. To me, what I do is priority and it's what I love doing. Music is the thing that keeps me together. It's like a shield for me – my musical abilities. I can fend off all kinds of things. So it's like a battle all the time, but I don't mind as long as I win through and seem to get a little bit across. I've built a structure, a kind of musical belief in myself, and that keeps me going.

This is in my blood. The only thing I can do is to write music and perform, and that's what I'm going to be doing – I think that's what *all* of us are going to be doing – until we die. If I didn't do this, I don't have anything else to do. I can't cook, and I'm not very good at being a housewife. I seem to have been doing this for so long now that I don't know what else to do. I'd be very vulnerable and I wouldn't know what to do, so I think I just have to keep doing it.

It's not a question of *having* to keep doing it, of course – I've made a lot of money and I could live beautifully and wonderfully for the rest of my life – but the way I live is that I have to be doing something every day. I have a nervous energy that needs to be doing something. There's a voice inside me saying, "Slow down, you'll burn yourself out!" but I can't stop. It's just a nervous energy that I have. I basically write music and I want to keep doing that. I have a lot of songs and I enjoy doing them. You see, it's come to a stage where before, I felt it was my work, my job, and though it's still my work now, I don't *have* to do it. I feel it's something I enjoy doing and it's very interesting. There are still lots of challenges ahead and I'm going to receive them with open arms.

Underneath it all, we like each other and we like the music we make. That's basically it. And if we didn't like the music, we'd say goodbye to each other.

I really wouldn't know about things in 20 years time. It would be nice if people were still buying our records then. I would hate to be doing it just to sell records and make money. We do it because we have interest in it, and if I lost that I would go and do something else. I like trying out different things, and at the moment there is a lot within Queen we can do. One day I might say to myself, "I have done enough with Queen so now I will do something else," but I couldn't tell you whether that will happen tomorrow or in two years time or in another ten years. Let's wait and see.

At this point in time I'm just having a good time. I just want to do things my way, and I want to have fun doing it. At the moment I don't think I'd like to tour. It's going back to that thing about wanting to break the format. As far as I'm concerned, I've been in the studio for two years – having done the Queen album [*The Miracle*, 1989] and before that the Montserrat album – and I just think it wouldn't be right for me. I feel it would be back to exactly what we said we wouldn't be doing.

I think it's just a matter of time. We've just got to wait and see. Then if something comes up and we decide that we want to tour, we will do it. But I personally didn't want to tour on the same pretext as before – that here comes an album so we go out on the road again. As far as I'm concerned we've done all those big venues and everything, we've got to think of something different now. Over the last years all we've done is a studio album per year and then tour and go around the world, and then by the time we come back we have to think of the next album.

For us to get to this level, for us to actually be here after all this time... I think we would have never arrived at this point if we hadn't taken those two years off [1987/88]. I really do. It's actually stepping outside of Queen, doing something else, and realising that we miss Queen and that we want to come back and do something new, is why I think this album [*The Miracle*] sounds so fresh.

We are four people with very different ideas, and it does need four people to actually want to do it. If one person doesn't want to tour, then you can't. I think I'm the actual spanner in the works at the moment, and I'll be very honest in saying so. I'm the one that doesn't want to tour.

I don't think I'm letting the others down, or anything. It's just that if one of them didn't want to do this album, then we would have to agree, because there's no point forcing somebody, especially after all these years. It would be so awful. You have to be hungry to do it – what we have done all these years. I'd hate to do that sort of *slogging* thing, for the sake of doing it. I mean, we don't need any more money, so we don't do it for the money. I think we do it for the music, which I know is a boring thing to say, but we do it because we still have the music in us.

Sometimes I think there must be more to life than rushing round the world like a mad thing. I can't carry on rocking the way I have done in the past – it's all too much. It's no way for a grown man to behave. I have stopped my nights of wild partying but that's not because I'm ill, but down to age. I'm no longer a spring chicken. Now I prefer to spend my time at home. It's part of growing up – this is what growing up is about. I'm trying to rest and calm down a bit.

I've always been serious, but I still have a flippant nature. I suppose being 39, you look upon it in a more sedate way. It's something that I instinctively don't think about. I also think that if you worry about it too often it does actually age you. I'm not worried about wrinkles and things like that. I don't get up every morning and rush to the mirror and see how many lines I've got. That's the best way to do it as far as I'm concerned. I don't worry. I mean, you're going to get old, you'll look old, and that's the way it is, no matter how many creams you use. It's just not me. There's nothing one can do about it. I'm not afraid of looking old. It's how you feel inside that matters. It sounds so clichéd, I know. And I am not worried about getting fat, in fact I'd love to put on a bit of weight and be a bit plump.

I'm not bad for 39 – not bad at all. And no facelift. There are probably people looking for tucks when they lift my hair back, but no, there are none of the Michael Jacksons here!

I don't know how other people are, but I don't worry about my age at all because I know I look beautiful anyway. Why should anybody worry about age? You can't do anything about it, you can't get younger. I'm not worried about getting any younger or older, I just want to live life to the full and spend my life doing wonderful things. I just don't worry about it. I think that age can be a good quality because age equals experience and I'm using all the experience I have gathered over the years to benefit from.

I'm perfectly fit and healthy, but of course I'm concerned about my health. Isn't everybody?

I pray I'll never get AIDS. So many friends have it. Some have died, others won't last much longer. I'm terrified that I'll be the next. Immediately after I have sex I think, "Suppose that was *the one*? Suppose the virus is now in my body?" I jump in the shower and try to scrub myself clean although I know it's useless.

I was totally devastated when I heard about my friends who have died from AIDS. It brought the seriousness of the illness home to me. I learnt the hard way. When you're young it is so much harder. I was thinking the other day, we were lucky to have sown our wild oats when we did, but they are just starting out. It is something the young have got to get to grips with.

I used to live for sex but now I've changed. I've stopped going out, stopped the nights of wild partying. I've almost become a nun. It's amazing, I thought sex was a very important thing to me but now I realise I've just gone completely the other way. Once, I was extremely promiscuous, it was excess in every direction, but now I'm totally different. I have stopped all that and I don't miss that kind of life. Everything is fine.

You see, I'm one of those people that can go from black to white. I don't like intermediary measures. It's quite easy for me to completely give up things. I can give up alcohol at the drop of a hat. AIDS has frightened me to death and so I've just stopped having sex. I just like titillation now. I'm into titillation. It's much more fun. What more can I do? I've stopped having sex and started growing tulips!

You can't expect people to just abstain from sex forever. I think the message of safe sex is essential and crucial. Anyone who sleeps around should have an AIDS test.

It is a very, very serious thing we are dealing with. I think people have to wait now, better times are ahead. This thing about safe sex is all very worthwhile, but you can still have fun. You can't expect people to just give up sex. People get freaked, they think they have AIDS and they shoot themselves, and then people find out that they didn't have it after all. People should be careful, but not get paranoid.

We're living with it now and it's there, on your doorstep, and you'd be a fool to say that you haven't heard of it. You can't get away from it. But if you get into the nitty-gritty of it, there are friends of mine who have died of AIDS. It's devastating.

How much more can one harp on about it? I am not the saviour of the fucking thing! I like those television ads where it says everybody is equal with AIDS – like money doesn't mean anything. AIDS is not prejudiced. AIDS is not prejudiced about who you are or what you do. It gets you!

Before, I was very greedy. I was promiscuous, that's true, but I've stopped all that because practicality came into it. You know what I'm talking about. It's up to the individual. Most people live by sex, but a lot of people can't do without it. A lot of people just have it as a pastime. I don't want to suddenly say that sex is boring or overrated because that would be farcical – having just said that I was very promiscuous, that would be a contradiction.

It sounds like I'm putting sex on a pedestal, but I'm not. You see, I took sex with everything I was doing. To me it was like a high. Everything was open to me, sex was a very integral ingredient to what I was doing. It was a very major factor in a lot of things I did. But I would never have thought of sex and nothing else. I was living life to the full and there was excess in every direction. There was also music of course. I had all that. I was weighing everything up together and I was living what one would call a very full life in every direction. Why not?

I have a very good relationship now and also I'm an old bird now, so the word *solace* came into it. You can't say you have a life of solace and go round fucking half the world. And I don't miss it. I really don't.

Like I've said before, I think that in the end being natural and being genuine is what wins. I'm not worried about making mistakes, I think I'm too old for that. This is a survival test.

There will come a point where there will be a unanimous vote, or whatever, when we feel instinctively that Queen have gone as far as they can go and there's nothing left, constructively or creatively. And the last thing I want to do is actually force things within Queen. I'd rather leave it at a nice level, and then do something completely different. And I'm sure that all of us have that kind of way of thinking.

I know there will be a time when I have to stop, but music will still be my thing, so I'll have to think in terms of what I *can* do. I don't want to end my life just being a rock'n'roll star. Maybe I can go into record production or I'll still write songs – because one might not have the physical fitness to run around on stage, but you can still write songs. So, one way or another the music side is always going to be in my life.

You can become very blasé, I know, but in a way it becomes harder because now it's a question of staying power. You've achieved everything, so what else is there? But the thing is, I've got nothing else to do, so I can't stop doing what I'm doing. I could live on the money I have for the rest of my days, but I'm not that kind of person. I want to work because I get bored.

I love the fact that I make people happy, in any form. Even if it's just half an hour of their lives, in any way that I can make them feel lucky or make them feel good, or bring a smile to a sour face, that to me is worthwhile.

I really don't want to change the world. To me happiness is the most important thing – to be happy and to have fun. If I'm happy it shows in my work. I take notice of everything, but in the end I just do things how I feel. I listen to advice, but I can't listen to everybody otherwise I just wouldn't be myself. In the end you are your own boss and you crack the whip, which is a very vulnerable position to be in. This is my life, I'm the boss and that's the only way I know how to be. I listen to criticism and advice but then I have to make up my own mind. In the end, all the mistakes and all the excuses are down to me. I can't pass the buck. I like to feel that I've just been my honest self and as far as I'm concerned I just want to pack in as much of life and fun as I can within the years that I have.

Will my music stand the test of time? I don't give a fuck! I won't be around to worry about it. In 20 years time… I'll be dead darlings. Are you mad?

I don't expect to make old bones, and what's more I don't really care. I certainly don't have any aspirations to live to 70. It would be so boring. I will be dead and gone long before that. I won't be here. I'll be starting a new life somewhere else – growing my own pomegranates.

I don't want to be a burden on anybody else. I would like to feel that I went without having to be a burden on anyone, and that's not condescending. I just don't want to. It's the honest truth. I'd love to go while I'm still on top.

I'm not going be like Eva Peron. I don't want to go down in history as one of those people who worried... hoping they realise, after I'm dead, that I created something or I invented something. Life is for living. I don't give a damn about all that. In the meantime, I've had fun and I want to go on having fun – doing this.

I don't want to sound morbid. 70 is a long way away. As far as I'm concerned I've lived a full life and if I'm dead tomorrow I don't give a damn. I've lived. I really have done it all.

If I'm dead and I want to be buried with all my treasures, like Tutankhamen, I'll do it. If I want a pyramid in Kensington, and I can afford it, I'll have it. Wouldn't that be fab?

Will I get to heaven? No. I don't want to. Hell is much better. Look at all the interesting people you're going to meet down there!

C'est la vie!

When I'm dead, I want to be remembered as a musician of some worth and substance. I don't know how they will remember me. I haven't thought about that – dead and gone. No, I haven't thought about it. I don't really think, "My God! When I'm dead are they going to remember me?" It's up to them. When I'm dead, who cares? I don't!

~THE END~

"Thank you, God bless and sweet dreams... you lot of tarts!"

ACKNOWLEDGMENTS

Simon and Greg offer sincere thanks to: Lucy Batcup, Jim Beach, Tildy Beach, Victor Blanke, Jer Bulsara, Anthony Cauchi, Alexi Cory-Smith, Helen Donlon, James Harman, Tom Jackson, Jim Jenkins, John Libson, Louise Lupton, Anne Meyer, Janice Page, Robin Rees, Amin Saleh, Jacky Smith, Jim Stevenson, Phil Symes, Gary Taylor, Nick Weymouth, David Wigg. And appreciation to John Deacon, Brian May, Roger Taylor and Freddie Mercury.

Is This The World We Created lyrics by kind permission of Queen Music Ltd. / EMI Music Publishing Ltd.

CREDITS

Books: *Freddie Mercury and Queen* – Neville Marten & Jeffrey Hudson (Faber & Faber), *Living On The Edge* – David Bret (Robson Books), *Queen: An Official Biography* – Larry Pryce (Star Books), *The Complete Guide To The Music of Queen* – Peter K Hogan (Omnibus Press), *The New Visual Documentary* – Ken Dean (Omnibus Press), *Queen: In Their Own Words* – Mick St. Michael (Omnibus Press), *Queen Live: A Concert Documentary* – Greg Brooks (Omnibus Press), *Freddie Mercury* – Peter Freestone & David Evans (Omnibus Press), *Freddie Mercury: A Kind of Magic* – Ross Clarke (Kingsfleet Publications), *Freddie Mercury: The Definitive Biography* – Lesley-Ann Jones (Hodder & Stoughton), *The Show Must Go On* – Rick Sky (Citadel Press), *As It Began* – Jim Jenkins & Jacky Gunn (Sidgwick & Jackson), *The Truth Behind The Legend* – David Evans & David Mimms (Britannia Press), *Queen: An Illustrated Biography* – Judith Davis (Proteus Publishing),

Magazines and newspapers: *Classic Rock, Record Hunter, Q, Daily Mirror, Disc, Daily Mail, The Sun, Mojo, NME (New Musical Express), Melody Maker, Circus, Record and Popswop Mirror* (aka Record Mirror), *Sounds*.

Photographs:
Jer and Bomi Bulsara, Brian May, Neal Preston, Richard Young/Rex Features, Simon Fowler, Denis O'Regan, Peter Röshler, Peter Hince, Terry O'Neill, Harry Goodwin, EMI Photo Archive, The Mark & Colleen Hayward Archive 2006, The Bolton Evening News, Naoaki Matsumoto, Douglas Puddifoot.

Index: Georgina Heatley

INDEX